A guided quest to authentic living

GOING
META

Thinking
about
thinking

PERSONAL CLARITY
SOCIAL HONESTY
HOLISTIC GROUNDING

Elsa Simpson

Designed by Out of the Blue Creative Communication Solutions
Cover design by Out of the Blue Creative Communication Solutions

Printed and bound by Print on Demand 5 Koets Street, Parow Industria 7493

First edition, first print 2020

ISBN 978 1 77616 099 0

This one's for you, Aletta.

"I took a deep breath and listened to the old brag of my heart. I am, I am, I am."

– SYLVIA PLATH

Contents

STAGE 2: Twist your trunk

Postscript 147

Acknowledgements 149

Addendums 155

Foreword

Before I first met Nico Simpson and then his wife Elsa in 2012, I had been travelling with the Organic ScoreCard (OSC) for more than nine years. Originally developed as a complex questionnaire with open answers, I transformed the OSC into an online questionnaire, with an extensive set of graphs as a result. It was still complicated to explain, therefore reserved for capable, well-trained coaches. But, as I always said, "The only way to do justice to the complexity of a person is a complex description".

I have personal experience with the complexity of the OSC. Originally I am a business strategist, but I had to take major steps in my development to be able to follow the ever-expanding depth of the instrument. This resulted in a decision to study psychoanalysis from 2006 to 2008 which was an important part and milestone in understanding the full breadth and depth of insight gained from the OSC.

The knowledge I had gained during the psychoanalysis study also heralded the last major change in the formulation of the OSC statements. Between the completion of my study in 2008 and meeting with the Simpsons, there were four years of patient and technically extensive personal feedback to clients, both business and private. Another consequence of the psychoanalysis training was that for the first time I gained insight into the identity of "team consciousness" – an almost tangible personality that could make or break the effectiveness and collaboration possibilities of a team.

Nico was in my first Organic Coach training group at Stellenbosch University in February 2012. Remarkably intelligent and critical, he was making drawings all the time during class. When I asked him what he was drawing and why, he indicated that he could only understand something if he could draw it: he had made a kind of comic strip from my teaching material! During those days he remained so critical, almost provocatively, that I became convinced that he would soon be lost as a student. The opposite turned out. The material had touched him in such a way that he was upset by it, but in a positive way. As a result, his wife Elsa took part in the April 2012 training group.

Elsa presented herself as a seasoned business coach, who had already seen a lot (also from other methodologies) and therefore constantly asked relevant and in-depth questions. Her thinking and working direction was continuously aimed at her customers: How could they use the theory and practice of the OSC? So Elsa soon came up with alternative presentation proposals: "If you change this into that, then my customers can do something with it!" Like her husband, Elsa turned out to be a deeply honest person with a warm heart for people and a great urge to help people when they need it.

The meeting with these two complementary professionals has greatly changed the Organic ScoreCard in terms of form and possibilities for expression. It now comes with drawings, symbols, archetypes, and with shorter and clearer explanations. It also has new areas of application. Nico and Elsa appeared to know the language of the customer. As a result, the Organic ScoreCard has turned into an instrument with easier access to larger groups of people, inside and outside the business community. The same applies to the field of team coaching. This duo's input in the use of the Organic ScoreCard in South Africa and in Europe has been significant.

Going Meta has become an impressive book in which readers are taken step by step along the 12 consciousness fields from the OSC. With extensive exercises and carefully chosen texts, readers get the chance to take their personal development to the next level. Everything is presented in an attractive and appealing way, which means that I can only conclude with: *Going Meta* is a book that you would grant everyone! With pride and joy I hand you over, readers of this book, to this amiable and highly knowledgeable author! Enjoy the book and its teachings. In the meantime, see the steps you take in your personal growth!

Marc Grond
Saint Médard-la Rochette, France

Prescript

Nico, my husband, has guided many students, authors and friends on their journeys to put their thoughts on paper.

During a break in Sedgefield, it dawned on me that Nico could do the same for me. He could help me write a book.

His involvement also made sense because I intended to base the book on the Organic Theory, which we discovered together. Nico is also the one who formed a very special friendship with Marc Grond, inventor of the Organic Theory and the Organic ScoreCard. Together, they have spent many dinners, walks and trips to philosophise about and dissect this rich theory until we could use it in a practical way in our journeys with people. They formulated the theory on awareness in a way that inspired people.

I am privileged to have a soul mate, husband, thinking partner and colleague all in one. These roles often get blurred, but it is in this fusion that we get creative. This book is a testimony to our innovative collaboration. In this book, you will meet him through many of his stories and experiences.

It would not have been possible to write this book without him.

Elsa Simpson

Introduction

> *"Awareness allows us to get outside of our mind and observe it in action."*
> – DAN BRULE

Meta awareness

This book is about going meta with awareness. You are invited on a journey to think about your thinking. To become aware of your awareness.

The Greek prefix *meta* means "after" or "beyond". In the common use of the word, *metadata* is "data about data", *metacognition* is "cognition about cognition" and a *metajoke* is "a joke about jokes". "This sentence contains 36 letters" is a metasentence because it is a sentence about a sentence, referring to itself.

"Going meta" is a more recent use of *meta* as a stand-alone term for the rhetorical trick of taking a conversation to another level of abstraction, for example when someone says, "This conversation is not going anywhere".

At the end of one of our training sessions in South Africa one of the participants remarked, "In the past, when I tried to think about how I think, everything just turned to wool in my mind. This framework gives me a roadmap to think about my thoughts." This book gives you a way of thinking about your thoughts.

Going Meta is a self-help book. The book was written to help people who are in a personal rediscovery process. It is aimed at helping people to re-assess whether the way they take on life is still working for them, and to unblock the flow to their authentic selves through guided teaching and exercises. The book assists people to get personal clarity, develop social honesty and experience holistic grounding. We explore the connection between rediscovering the authentic self and a creative life, and the experience of flow.

The 12 aspects of awareness

Our approach guides readers through 12 aspects of awareness, unlocking unexplored awareness potential. This can unblock the bottlenecks restricting your innovative flow and open up opportunities for self-discovery and authentic living. Not only do we explore the range of awareness but together we go on a quest to discover who you are and who you want to be.

These 12 aspects of awareness are like a lighthouse with 12 different windows. We invite you into your own lighthouse and try to 'tempt' you to open all the different windows. We ask you to open them one by one so that your light can shine through and light up the view. Slowly, one window per week, your light will start to beam in different directions. Some windows of awareness are already wide open, allowing you to simply enjoy the view. Some windows have never been opened, calling for some effort to open them. Sometimes this new view will take your breath away, and you will discover this amazing unexplored picture for the first time. Sometimes the view will be blurry and you struggle to see through the fog. All of this is fine. Focus your eyes for one week only and move on to the next window. All these windows look in the direction of your authentic self. In other words, even though some weeks are more difficult than others, just keep going. Some weeks will be a celebration while some will offer a steep learning curve.

People who went on this journey experienced it in different ways. For example, there was a teacher whose husband had lost his job. All the uncertainties about their future made her feel insecure. She dared to open the window to "My Grounding: being my own best friend" for the first time. On her journey through the book she recognised her fears about the future. Then she discovered that certainty is an illusion and started practising peace of mind in the moment through some of the exercises (in Chapter 3). To her surprise, every now and then she got glimpses of the peace of mind that she could hold on to. She discovered that if she continued to accept the present moment, embracing her authentic self, her husband did not have to deal with her anxiety. At the same time, new opportunities unfolded on his side. She started to experience what it means to be your own best friend. She loved it. It was difficult for her to move to the fourth window and she grieved over her newfound "best friend" during the next week. She was learning to love herself.

A facilitator who struggled with "My Grounding" was very relieved to move to "My Friendship" – a window that was very wide open in his life. Being a natural relationship builder, he enjoyed Chapter 4, reinforcing his own gifts of bringing people together in large crowds.

Your journey with and through this book will be unique. Receive each week as it comes to you. Plunge into it and then move on. Do not stay with a chapter for longer than a week.

The rhythm of life

The flow of this journey is based on an ancient rhythm of life. It is therefore important to follow the chronological sequence of the book. Be mindful of what you are reading and working with in the book, and how this is reflected in your life and the world around you. This is not only a journey through the book, but a journey through life. Let life and the book be in conversation with one another. Many people who have done this journey commented on the synchronicities they had experienced between the two.

One lady explained that the week she started chapter 6 (My Creativity) she 'accidentally' met her kindergarten teacher for the first time since school. The teacher recalled what a natural genius she was as a little girl in her class. The teacher also reminded her of a national competition they had won (with the teacher as coach), and how good she was in maths and music. The teacher ended by saying: "You were always an old soul with lots of wisdom far beyond your age!" For this lady, this correlated perfectly with the week's reading and exercises.

Another reader was in between jobs. When she opened herself up to building relationships with new people, after working through My Friendship in Chapter 4, new career opportunities were presented to her.

Flow

"The only way to make sense out of change is to plunge into it, move with it, and join the dance."
– ALAN WILSON WATTS

The closer you live to your authentic self, the more flow you will experience. According to the Hungarian-American psychologist Csíkszentmihályi, flow is when you are intensely focused in the present moment. When this happens, what you are doing and your thoughts and ideas merge into one. You feel that you have the potential to succeed. You are no longer self-consciously reflecting on yourself. You have a sense of personal control over the quest you are undertaking. Time feels different. It is as if it is moving very slowly and very fast at the same time. You are engrossed in who you are and what you are doing. Just being and doing has an intrinsic reward. This is flow.

Spending time in flow is about living authentically. It leads to positive effects and better performance.

Going Meta is an invitation to join the journey, and to become free to be completely involved in what you are doing. To focus and to concentrate. To risk living outside everyday reality and embrace moments of ecstasy.

This journey promises inner clarity. It is about knowing what needs to be done. Knowing that your dream is doable and your skills adequate for the task at hand. It is about having a sense of serenity in this quest. Tackling scary mountains without worrying about yourself. Feeling how you grow beyond the boundaries of your own skin.

Authentic living is being in your flow while keeping your centre. That is when you are fully alive. Aliveness is playing to your strengths without being imprisoned by the anxious inner voices of your past, the demanding outer voices of your present or the scary voices of your future.

You are the instrument that makes the music in your life. When the instrument is in tune, it plays beautiful music. Life tunes the instrument.

Authentic self

*"There is a crack, a crack in everything.
That's how the light gets in."*
– LEONARD COHEN

In *Going Meta* we share exercises and activities, and prompt you to explore each dimension of awareness. *Going Meta* is a guided programme for personal renewal. It will help you discover your authentic self, and take the steps you need to gain personal clarity, social honesty and holistic grounding.

An authentic self has personal clarity. This quest will not only help you to know who you really are, but it will also invite you to show this to the outside world. Personal clarity has to do with your understanding of your history and your ability to be open to receive what is coming your way.

An authentic self has social honesty. Living honestly in community means we are connected to people; we are a gift to them. Together we live in an environment that supports us through structures and negotiated agreements.

Lastly, an authentic self has a holistic grounding. Our quest will lead you to a place where you will be able to be in the moment because you have access to your roots, earlier generations and creativity.

Leonard Cohen, the legendary Canadian poet and singer, did not like to explain his music. He made a rare statement about "Anthem" on The Future Radio Special. Many people believe "Anthem" is one of his most beautiful and hopeful songs.

According to Cohen, this song is not about perfection as "... there is a crack in everything ... that's how the light gets in". And that is where the resurrection is and where the return and the repentance is. It starts with the confrontation, with the brokenness of things.

"I don't know my place in life!"

"I'm not myself."

"I don't like myself!"

"I can't connect with others!"

These are some of the statements people typically make when they become aware that they are out of touch with their authentic self. Our self-understanding is often a costume we have been wearing ever since we adopted the thoughts, feelings and behaviours projected onto us by parents, caregivers, family and society. Your 'costume' can act, think and even feel. You can do that because you have transferred your sense of who you are to the costume. You have worn it for so long that you think it is who you are.

But all along, our authentic self is showing through the small cracks in the costume. Perhaps we feel it as a deep longing for something. Maybe we are surprised by something we have said or done. Possibly, we are just slowly discovering new aspects of ourselves that we have been ignoring for some time.

False self

We also mention the false self on the journey. This is a quest towards our authentic self, but sometimes it shows up as false reflection. It usually appears under stress or during trauma. Sometimes it stays and becomes part of our life strategy. For example, a person with natural inspiring energy can also tend to seek attention or withdraw. A person who plays a stabilising role in a group or community can become rigid. People with natural trust in their makeup can occasionally trust too much and become naive. We hope that by recognising the anxieties and traits of the false self, you will find another avenue to your authentic self.

Your authentic self is who you are meant to be while your false self is who the world is trying to force you to be. Sometimes people urge you to do YOU. However, you must first understand that doing YOU does not mean doing more of your 'costume'. It means discovering and living in and from the authentic self.

Embracing your authentic self means living from a deep sense of who you are. There is a unique and unquestionable power in becoming and being your true self.

Going Meta guides you to be comfortable in your own (original) skin.

Once you re-discover your real self you become comfortable with who you truly are.

You have one priceless life to live. You are called upon to spend it living your true destiny.

The basic tools

Meta Moments: Daily journaling

"Awareness is like the sun. When it shines on things, they are transformed."

– NHAT HANH

This 12-week programme invites you to actively participate in daily journaling. This is a loosely structured writing ritual that will help you to "go meta". Through journaling, you can clear your mental clutter.

Daily journaling can help you to become aware of your inner drive, as well as your acquired behaviours. Over time, it will reveal the brain strategy you are maybe not aware of. This will deepen your insight into your intrinsic motivation. It will also help you appreciate and validate your current strengths.

Writing down your thoughts is a proven technique to harness your creative ideas and skills. Some people do three pages of longhand, stream-of-consciousness writing every morning. This helps to declutter their minds, and to recognise the things that are in the forefront of their brains.

Keeping a journal creates a permanent record of your feelings, shifts in your environment and "facts" about events in your life. This allows you to look back on important life events and rediscover how you felt at the time.

This can be a reflective learning experience. By reading about your past experiences, you will be able to see how you have grown or matured. This can help to bring things into perspective.

This habit of journaling will enable you to develop an action plan for a growth trajectory. Furthermore, it will help you to identify growth areas and make real-time awareness interventions possible.

When journaling, you may think about three things daily:

1. The "facts" as objectively as possible (Captain's log)

2. The shifts in the environment you have experienced (Diary)

3. The emotions you felt (Debriefing).

Captain's log

Write down the facts of what happened.

Write down what actually happened without adding any interpretation, adjectives, emotions or explanations.

Everything is a chance to gain clarity about your authentic self – every place you go, every person you meet, every place you work, everything you do, every conversation you have, every mistake you make, every success you achieve, every conversation you overhear ...

Write them down.

Life is the classroom. If you pay attention, you will learn the lessons. Every day is a new page in your textbook. If you have the mentality of a student, your training has already begun.

Example:

"I did not bring work home yesterday."

"I had a conversation with my boss. She asked me to redo the report."

"I said no."

Diary

The diary differs from the captain's log in that the captain's log is about clinical facts while the diary is about the experience of movement or stability in and around you.

In your diary, describe any shifts you have experienced. The shifts can be in your environment or routines. Write down what gives you a feeling of things are getting more stable, or things are moving. This can be around you or inside you.

We often think of discovering our authentic selves as something that comes to us. We expect an epiphany that arrives when we least expect it. But the truth is, in some ways, it is already happening. It has already begun. You already have some sense of what you should do with your life, even if it is not clear right now. The trick is to spot the direction hidden in your life.

Shifts can either be towards stability or away from it. If you get stuck, read through the following list and see what comes to mind:

Shifts in me

How I react to life in general is changing.

My understanding of my past is changing.

My understanding of who I am is changing.

What I show of myself to other people is changing.

Shifts in we

What I think I bring to others is changing.

How we connect to each other is changing.

Who we work together is changing.

How we structure our environment is changing.

Shifts in all the rest

Where I fit in is changing.

How we do things around here is changing.

How we understand things is changing.

How I approach uncertainty is changing.

When you write about a shift happening around you, acknowledge this. Give recognition to the prompts on your path. We all have some sort of gut feeling of what we are supposed to do with our lives or what parts of our lives we need to rediscover. What we need is not necessarily a map but rather a shovel. Often, what will help us the most is a set of tools to dig and discover. Writing about any shifts in your life is an excellent shovel.

Example:

"I am taking control of my private life."

"The discussion with my boss played out differently. She seemed to be more open to my suggestions."

"I did not bring work home yesterday which normally would make me feel guilty, but yesterday I felt free."

Debrief

Describe your emotions and the intensity of these emotions.

Here you could use the Emotional Grid (Addendum 1) to help you identify the specific emotions you have experienced.

For examples see Addendum 2.

Example:

"It feels liberating to push back on all the demands."

"I felt appreciated and listened to."

"I immediately felt sooo sorry for her, I stopped smiling and was emotionally touched."

Your journaling can cover all three or any of these aspects.

To maintain this habit or discipline is not always easy. Whenever I start to journal in the morning, a long list of things that I need to do for my work, my family and the household pops up. It makes such a noise in my head that I cannot hear myself think. So I have developed the habit of writing this list down on the left side of my journal (I journal on the right side). Some days the to-do list seems to weigh more than my journaling. On those days I never get around to journaling and just start doing all these things – quickly send that email while it is still early as it will help me so much later on during the day …

Tasks can distract you. However, other people can distract you too. When I took a break to work on this book, my family, friends and clients started to phone me about all sorts of matters that were urgent to them – things that required my attention. Most of the time I find it easier to direct my passion and drive towards things and people rather than towards myself. But, when I do manage to use it to focus on my inner landscape, magical things happen. This is reminiscent of when an air hostess on an airplane explains the safety procedures. Passengers are advised to put on their own oxygen masks before attending to children and elders. In life there are times when caring for yourself first is the best way to have the capacity to care for others.

Three stages

Another metaphor that guided me in the structure of this book was the tree with its roots, trunk and crown. Therefore, the first four weeks will focus on your roots. The next four weeks will explore your trunk while the last four weeks will examine your crown.

Wiggle your roots

We will therefore start with your roots – the basis of your being. Your roots will help you feel that you have the right to exist. They give you the necessary support. They show you where you stand in life and with other people.

We have learned from people doing this process that if your roots have not yet been developed as strongly as the rest of your tree, you may struggle during the first stage of this journey. We encourage you to push through. We promise it gets better.

We often need to encourage people to keep going during the first four weeks. If you find the first weeks difficult, consider getting help. Look for a coach or therapist if needed or simply focus on the bits and pieces you do enjoy and move on, week by week. Even small alterations in your roots will bring huge growth or strengthening in your tree. In other words, do not let struggling discourage you. Trust that you will learn what you need to learn during this stage in your life and move forward.

Twist your trunk

The second set of affirmations will strengthen your trunk. Your trunk awareness empowers and structures you. You will experience power that directs your life and structures your being. You will become aware of the consistency of the outer and inner life themes from your past.

Wave your crown

The third set of affirmations has to do with your reactions to change and fitting in. This awareness will help you to think about movement in you and others. It also guides you to become aware of what you show in terms of what is being asked of you.

An appreciative approach

Between all the explanations and stories you will discover a few explicit and implicit assumptions.

The first overarching assumption is that we believe you will make better progress if we can help you appreciate who you are and the journey you have travelled so far. Rather than working with a "gap model" where we show you everything you are

NOT doing, we want to guide you to discover where you are succeeding. We will help you to see where you are already embracing your authentic life. This journey will highlight where in the past you have been true to who you are or to who you are meant to be. We will help you to identify the things you are already "doing right" in order to empower you to carry on and move forward.

No one reacts positively to "critical instructions". The truth is, many of us have internalised criticism, which creates shame or leaves us paralysed. An appreciative approach embraces the core of who we are without any judgement. This is the most effective approach to growth.

Guidelines for the journey

- Open yourself up to this journey and expect to be transformed.
- Spend one week per chapter, reading and doing the exercises (as many or as few as you want to). After a week, move on whether you are done or not.
- Reflect at the end of every week. This can be done individually, with a coach or in a group.
- Try to journal as many days of the week as possible.
- Look out for clues in your environment that are synchronised with your journey.
- Stay in the chronological rhythm of the journey.
- Consult a coach or therapist when you get stuck. It can help you to gain clarity.

Guidelines for groups traveling together

See Addendum 5 on page 165 for the Group Discussion Guide.

Some people find it helpful to do this journey in a group context as the group structure helps to keep them accountable. Find a partner or up to six people (not more) to join you in this journey. The group sessions can be face-to-face or virtual (online sessions allow people to join remotely).

Agree on the following rules of engagement:

- Commit to the above-mentioned *Guidelines for the journey*.
- Commit to weekly timeslots for 12 consecutive weeks. Sessions typically last one to two hours.
- Follow the rule of 'equal airtime' for each group member.
- Listen. Do not give advice or rescue other members. Respect the individual journeys and insights.
- Empathise and validate each other's insights and experiences of the previous week.
- Celebrate and appreciate each other's effort and journey.
- Consider inviting a coach or facilitator to assist should the group get stuck.

STAGE 1

Wiggle your roots

The first four weeks of your journey will focus on your roots.

Your roots are the basis of your being. They help you feel that you have the right to exist. They give you the necessary support. They show you where you stand in life and where you stand with other people.

"A tree stands strong not by its fruits or branches, but by the depth of its roots."

– ANTHONY LICCIONE

ONE
Recognising the full worth of my existence

I have a place in this world.

Position – it is about my awareness in being

This week, you are invited to become aware of your place in the world. Like a sextant or GPS that helps you find your position in life, you are invited to seek your importance in your environment. This chapter will guide you so that you do not have the experience of feeling lost and disconnected from your environment. You will also be guided to discover how to be a reliable and responsible anchor point in your environment. You are invited to have peace of mind with the givenness of life.

"I visited many places, some of them quite exotic and far away, but I always returned to myself."
– DEJAN STOJANOVIC

I have a place in this world.
I am alert to the possibilities that life offers.

I do what I do because I am who I am.

I embrace the givenness of life.

What to expect this week:
Starting the journey

Your journey to authentic living starts today. The challenge of the first week is that you have a limited awareness of the journey that lies before you. Become aware of how your environment and inside are being shaken up. The pressure you are feeling is giving positive momentum to your story.

You are invited to face these beginnings of change. The pressure you are feeling is actually a call to action. It is the first stirring of your authentic self that wants to be reborn.

Over the next 12 weeks you will go on a quest that will take you from the known into a new world of awareness. This quest will help you discover large and unexplored awareness territories. These lands have gifts you have not yet received. This journey will make you question the status quo and expand your awareness.

A friend of ours regularly receives speeding tickets. The irony is that he does not speed. He drives 80 km/h everywhere he goes, unfortunately also in 60 km/h zones. That is how we often use our awareness. We have a fixed set of awarenesses we use without ever changing our speed. However, the situation determines the norm. Where you are driving determines your speed. What you are busy with determines your awareness. Your context should influence how you act or think.

This book will help you explore different ways of thinking. This will allow you to discover which ones will help you the most in your situation.

> *"He who completes a quest does not merely find something. He becomes something."*
>
> LEV GROSSMAN

My authentic existence

As I embrace my authentic existence I have peace of mind in the givenness of life.

I am free from the here and now.

The givenness of life is often experienced as a natural sense of long-term reassurance.

My being in life sometimes feels like destiny.

I am the personification of self-confidence and inner peace.

I have the ability to remain calm and collected on a fundamental level of being, even amidst turmoil.

My stability has an inviting kind of logic. Although it does not seem to flow from me, I am saturated with it.

My authentic existence radiates ease and natural flow, which even I sometimes find mystifying to understand.

Ⓐ Be alert to the possibilities that life offers

"I dwell in possibility ..."
– EMILY DICKINSON

Invitations to change

This week you will encounter two invitations to change. The first one is on a practical level, the second on an inner level.

At this early stage of your quest it could happen that someone challenges you on a practical level. Be on the lookout for someone challenging you, as if he or she is calling you to become part of an adventure. This calling could be bigger or outside the ordinary life you are now living. You could even be asked to "prevent an impending catastrophe" to yourself, your family or society at large. There could be a new threat, occasionally disguised as an opportunity, you are called to face. Someone, a messenger of the system in which you are living, could invite you to kick-start a new chapter in your life.

Paul Schrere tells of the day he went to the library to look up the assault of the Light Brigade during the Crimean War because he remembered that among the drums and guns, death and pain there was one woman who created space for people. He wanted to tell the story of this woman. All alone, lantern in her hand, she walked from bed to bed among the wounded. And soldiers kissed her shadow. He knew her name – Florence Nightingale. But however hard he tried, he could not remember what they fought for.

In the end, you will not remember what you feared and fought for. What remains will be the life you have lived.

On an inner second level you are invited to hear your need for change. This week you will be nudged to recognise your need to restore inner and external balance. This nudging may come as a dream, a new idea or a calling from life. Your false existence can be insecure and on the verge of critical self-doubt, fearing for your own survival. You may end up scanning and waiting without taking decisions.

The messenger will provide you with a practical challenge this week to continue on your journey. The message can be a person, a crisis event or simply an email. Be on the lookout for a "treasure map" arriving through the mail or a phone call from a long lost friend. Be open to a "chance encounter" or a passage in a book. Listen to your dreams and eavesdrop on conversations on the bus.

I know of a discussion between an editor and a man who reported to him. This man is a part-time videographer at a small community newspaper. The editor was explaining his need for regular video clips for his online platform. He needed someone who could take up this responsibility and run with it. He explained that the videographer's previous work was exactly the type of videos he was looking for. The editor expressed his frustration about the times nothing was produced. So he offered this position to the videographer, saying these videos would made a big difference. All the videographer needed to do was to take it. And I knew from previous discussions that the videographer wanted it.

What did the videographer do? He hesitated. He explained that he would rather get direct instructions and specific guidance. He said he probably needed more training on how to do this better. He listed all the ways in which he was not ready for this responsibility.

He had difficulty taking the position offered to him.

In our quest to live our authentic self, positions are given to us. We just need to receive them.

This week, be on the lookout for positions being offered to you: Be my friend, be my mentor, be the team leader, be my confidante ... Sometimes these positions are being offered to you. Sometimes initiatives you took are being validated by others. Embrace that position. Receive it. Embody it. Live it. Celebrate it.

The first position we all have in life is our birth position based on our family of origin. No one can take this away from you – this is given to you. Often, without you knowing it, you recreate this original position later on in life. Manfred Kets de Vries, a leadership coach, says we all recreate our family of origin in our work place (as an employee or team member as well as a leader or manager). Often, people are unconsciously aware of this. It can therefore bring a lot of light when they become aware of this position.

Questions for reflection

Each week, we will reflect on a number of core questions. The first question you will be exploring this week is: How can I seek my importance in my environment?

Become aware of the clues your environment is giving you about where you will find spaces to contribute.

Note down all the feedback you have received from your environment validating (even if it is in a crooked manner) your contributions.

B I do what I do because I am who I am

"My feeling is that labels are for canned food ...
I am what I am – and I know what I am."
– MICHAEL STIPE

The second question of this week is: How can I be a reliable and responsible anchor point in my environment?

The quest is to discover and embrace your authority in life.

Your false existence may have created fixed ideas you have about yourself. When this happens, you are unable to look at alternatives. You can become a grinding wheel, turning slowly, almost making no progress. You become unable to embrace your power.

One day I was sitting in a funky cubicle at a tech company when I heard very determined footsteps coming my way. I was surprised because the next person I needed to see was a young guy in his early twenties. In came a sturdy, very friendly young man who greeted me with a firm handshake. He looked me straight in the eyes. There was nothing tentative or uncertain about him.

I explained that I usually start a session with a question. I asked him whether he had a question, the answer of which would give him insight. He frowned and said, "A question. No, I don't really have questions." He continued to tell me that he completed his three-year degree in one year and started working six months ago. He really enjoys his work and he values the opportunity to work for this international company with all the wonderful prospects. Then he hesitated and said, "Perhaps this can help you with a question. The other day they did a personal development plan and the manager wanted to know whether I wanted to go into management or software development. That is something that I don't know at this stage!" He smiled, very glad that he could give me what I wanted. A question!

As the discussion continued, he started telling me the story about his position in his family. He was the only male in his extended family. His father died when he was three years old. Since he could remember, he was the man in the house for his mother and sisters, as well as for all his nieces. His uncle left when his nieces were still small. From a very young age he knew he needed to work hard to provide for one day. He made decisions in the best interest of his family long before he was supposed to do that. He took pride in the responsibilities he took on and in organising the people around him. The people in his extended family took his lead without hesitation. He never knew any other kind of position. Therefore, he is very well practised in this position. Becoming aware of this was a revelation to him, making his career choice so much easier.

He discovered, "Okay, yes, when I think about it, it actually is a no-brainer. I don't know how not to lead!"

As an afterthought, he told me that he is engaged and will get married in a few months' time. I was curious to know more. "So, what is your position in the relationship?"

With his beautiful open smile he said, "Now that is a good question! How did you know to ask this? The other day she asked me, 'Do you always need to make all the decisions?'" He laughed as he explained the 'fight' they had, while through his smile and bright eyes I could literally see how the penny dropped for him. He did not know any position other than leading.

"Here is your question for our next session: What position do I take in my relationship?" Greeting me, he laughed, "She is so going to love this story!"

Questions for reflection

Make a list of all the positions life has given you:

- Your position in your family (e.g., I am the second born)
- Your position in your current relationship network (e.g., I am the caring one)
- Your position at work (e.g., I am a programmer, I am a student)
- Your position in terms of your significant other(s) (e.g., I am a partner, a friend)
- Your position in your faith community or recreational communities (e.g., I am a small group leader; I am the goalie).

Next, complete each of the above-mentioned positional sentences with the words: "... therefore I have the authority to ..."

C Embrace the givenness of life

"Before I can tell my life what I want to do with it,
I must listen to my life telling me who I am."
– PARKER PALMER

Your disconnected false existence can dwell in the haziness of life and its meaning, unable to feel, understand or get moving. You then feel held (almost captive) in the invisible arms of your comfort zone.

The question you need to explore is: How can I have peace of mind with the givenness of life?

The other day I drove to a coffee shop in a shopping mall for a change of scenery. I wanted to do some journaling and then grab the necessary groceries on my way home. I had just settled in with my coffee and started to write when someone tapped me on the shoulder. "Hi, stranger, how are you?"

I looked up at the warm face of a mother with two kids, one on her hip and the other standing next to her. "I saw you in the parking lot and decided to come and look for you."

I greeted her while racking my brain to try and remember her name. I definitely knew her, but no name or context wanted to pop up. For a split second I panicked and then the file in my head opened up. It's Gillian. Of course, it's Gillian. How could I not recognise her! I had been thinking about her story quite a bit. I made a mental note to try and contact her to ask for her permission to use her story in this book and here she appeared out of nowhere.

After the usual "How are you?" questions, she told me that she was going for an interview the next day and that she was very nervous. She would really like to have this job. I then told her that I had been thinking of her a lot and that I wrote about her. She smiled and gestured with her hand, "I can't even remember that, but of course you can use the story".

I reminded her of the voice recording I made of our last contact. I was going to use it for research. I listened to it again, amazed by her wise insights. We checked that I still had the correct phone number and she left.

The next morning I left her a good luck voice note while quoting her own words back to her from a previous transitional period in her life: "I just wanted to remind you of what you said when looking for a job three years ago. You told me now that you know yourself better and appreciate your own gifts more. You said it is as if you are interviewing the organisation to check whether it will be a good fit for your gifts as much as they are interviewing you." She thanked me for this just-in-time note.

Later that day I received a joyful message telling me that the interview went well and that they wanted to appoint her because she was good at seeing patterns. What a wonderful fit!

She said to me that she told her husband she could not believe how the sequence of events played out the way it did. She was amazed at how much this natural flow of life supported her again during this transition.

I was thinking of her and then she showed up. She was nervous about a big step in her life and then I popped up in her life to remind her of a previous successful transition. It could not be by accident!

This happens when you open up to the adventure called life by letting your heart rest in the givenness of life.

> "It is only with the heart that one can see rightly; what is essential is invisible to the eye."
>
> — ANTOINE DE SAINT-EXUPÉRY, THE LITTLE PRINCE

Receive the givenness of life

At the beginning of your quest you were invited to receive the givenness of life. Below, we suggest different ways of doing this. Read through the options below and decide which ones you want to try.

1. Develop a sense of wonderment

Become aware of the beauty that is in and around you. For example, if you live in the countryside you can be in awe of the appeal of nature. If you reside in the city, you can admire the architecture.

2. Appreciate people

Observe the elusive gestures made by people. A gentle smile. A nod of encouragement. An act of kindness. Noticing this will increase your appreciation of being alive.

3. Practice present-moment awareness

Be in the moment. Stop and know the past is gone. Also, you cannot second-guess or control the future. You can only receive the here and now. In the present, there is no stress, only peace. Breathe deeply and gain an appreciation of the moment in which you exist.

4. Practice kind compassion

Give flowers. Babysit. Listen deeply. Arrange a surprise date. Embrace your destiny with self-confidence and gently let an act of kindness flow through you.

5. Boost your joy

Be mindfully present in the place given to you. Sit on the porch and watch the sun set. Be filled with awe. Stroll along the beach, barefoot. Feel the sand between your toes. Listen to the gulls. Feel the moment.

6. Show gratitude

Thank someone for his or her kindness. Point out character traits that you appreciate. Mindfully seek out positive aspects in the people around you.

7. Celebrate abundance

Instead of thinking about what you feel you need, celebrate your riches and abundance. Air your gratitude. Express your delight about having plenty of everything that you require in your life.

Mindfulness rhythm

Do mindful breathing

Actively breathe until you are aware of your breathing.

I am grateful for ...

Complete the sentence by listing old relationships, opportunities, wins of yesterday, amazing things you have achieved, things granted to you, experiences, and things around you. Write a thank you note.

I am ...

Complete the sentence with affirmations and strengths.

Task: Ask why questions

- If you often think about your place in the world, ask yourself: Why would I like to know what "act properly" is?
- If you almost never think about your place in the world, ask yourself: Why do I shut myself off from the world around me?

Reflection: Checking in on existence

- How often did you manage to do your journaling?
- What light bulb moments did you have?
- Where in the week did you experience a special moment?
- What did you struggle with?
- Where was your position affirmed?

For the more adventurous

- **Finger paint »** Finger painting isn't just fun for kids – adults can enjoy it as well. Get your hands messy and really have fun spreading paint around. Draw anything you like. The focus is on getting in touch with yourself.
- **Paint a rock »** This project is meant to offer you strength. One option is to paint on a rock things that empower you. The other is to paint the struggles you have overcome.

- **Huge colour blocks »** Draw something *huge*. Getting your body involved and moving around can help release emotions as you are drawing. Make big blocks of colour on you "canvas".

- **Commemorative document »** Document an experience where you did something you thought you could not do. This is a chance to commemorate a special moment in your life. Use any means you would like to explore.

- **Natural material »** Use natural materials to create something. Leaves, sticks, dirt, clay and other natural stuff can help you get in touch with the natural world and the more primal side of yourself.

TWO
Recognising the full worth of my inside

I feel good about myself.

Motivation – my inner being

This week, your meta journey continues. You are being asked to examine your deepest inner flame. You will explore your inner being and how you could use your passion and conviction to reinvent yourself. This could confront you with your anxiousness to survive as well as your feelings of not recognising yourself. You will also be asked to embrace the reliable core of who you are and have always been. This will guide you towards being an abundant source of rest for yourself and others.

> *"You find peace not by rearranging the circumstances of your life, but by realizing who you are at the deepest level."*
> – ECKHART TOLLE

I feel good about myself.

I am born beautifully. I am reinventing myself.

I am a reliable bearer of care.

I radiate inner confidence.

What to expect this week: Call to action

Week 2 is characterised by a growing feeling of the need to change. You are confronted with all the polarities in your life. You know of all the forces trying to claim your attention. These forces are pulling you in different directions and causing tension. By focusing on who you are, you could be struggling with the dilemma of celebrating yourself on the one hand and reinventing a new you on the other hand. Or you could be torn between trying to resist change and struggling to embrace your stable core. You could also be feeling the tension between not arrogantly looking down your nose at life and radiating inner confidence.

A Born beautifully – reinventing myself

> *"If you can give your child only one gift, let it be enthusiasm."*
>
> – BRUCE BARTON

The first question of this week is: How can I use my passion and conviction to reinvent myself?

Our quest starts with shifting the passion we sometimes use to please others towards reinventing ourselves in an authentic direction.

Directing your inner passion towards your environment creates a false inside. Your anxious false inside can feel threatened, anxious and mill around without really achieving anything. Then you start to fight for survival, like someone pushed into a corner.

A healthy call to action, however, can come from three directions. Script-writing guru Keith Cunningham calls them "the call from within", "the call from without" and "the call from below".

We invite you to explore the source of your unease. Each of these serve as internal energy to get you going on your quest.

You can be called from *within*. Here the energy for reinventing is an inner or self-initiated drive. Cunningham invites us to imagine a small hut in a tiny hamlet in the woods. In the hut is Little Hans who has grown up to be a big boy. When he stretches in the morning, his hands break through the roof of the cottage. His pants hardly go down to his knees. And when he flexes his muscles, the seams of his shirt split open. One day, he said to himself, "This hut is too small for me! This village is too small for me! There's a big world out there, and I must find my place in it."

If you feel like Little Hans, there is a strong internal impetus to move forward. This type of inner drive is often fed by idealism, hope or innocence.

Inner drive is not without its problems. It can be naively built on the assumption that you are in control of your destiny. You may be unaware of or blind to the trials awaiting you. In times of reinventing yourself it is important not to build on empty bravado. That will not protect you from the harshness of life. If you can connect deeply with your own beauty, you can enter the journey of "losing yourself".

When working with a client, my process usually starts with looking the person in the eye, seeing him or her as a person – a uniquely created human being. Over the years I have used different tools to help me see this person in front of me in order to validate his or her existence … the real "I".

We all have wonderful ways of disguising our real inside. Some hide behind a cloud of mystique. Others are very sure about who they are and who not. Many are so aware of what other people want them to be that they blurt out all their faults so that they can jump the gun on you shaming them. Sometimes you are so aware of everything that is not okay, and you so want to be loved, accepted and wanted that you do not dare to wait for the verdict. If someone then says something appreciative, you immediately dismiss it as being kind or diplomatic.

I identify with this last group. Perhaps that is why I prefer to start by looking at what is already good about a person. I first started doing it "undercover" because that was not supposed to be done by a professional person. The belief was that you need to confront constructively in order to provide the leverage for change. There are even lists of how to confront constructively.

I have had the opportunity of working with supervisors in a clothing factory. They were strong women, having survived the poor circumstances in which they grew up. They often started working illegally at the age of 13. They did this because there was no food on the table. They were tough. They had wisdom, even though they had very limited formal schooling.

We did feedback in groups. They had to appreciate themselves as well as the people around them. We had to lay down strong rules of appreciation. In their tough world, shaming was one of their tools of communication.

As soon as their beautiful existence was being validated, it was as if a dam wall just gave way! When the facilitator and the rest of the group reacted appreciatively, tears started flowing.

The appreciation of their existence in a caring and empathetic way was unbearable. Many of them have not experienced anything like this before. We could not really follow the prepared process as people spontaneously went straight into telling the stories of their existence of how they were born (often unwanted) and survived in a family with siblings and an extended family with too many people to be fed. Usually they had to live from the low income earned by a dominant woman in the household. The stories continued with the sadness of the alcohol and drug dependency and how this affected them as children. Many ended their stories with them now being strong women and the providers in the households.

To my surprise they came back the next morning (the second day of a three-day course) giving feedback on how their behaviour had changed. One of my favourite storylines was told, in different versions, by the almost a hundred women:

"Every day, as I am walking home from the railway station, I start shouting at my household to warn them that I am coming so that they can get things in order. Yesterday, I did not feel like shouting. I felt calm as I approached my house. I approached them in a kind and respectful voice, asking how their day was. They could not believe what was going on and some even asked if I was ill! At first it was very difficult for them to trust the 'peace', but gradually they started relaxing. We cooked food together and ended up chatting around the table."

Asking very curiously what had happened on the first day that made them act differently that evening, I got vague answers: "I was calm after the day and did not want to yell like usual." Or, "I don't really know. I just did not feel like being upset." And then, one day, one of the women said, "I understood I have all these beautiful things inside of me. You recognised it and then my team members recognised it. At first I could not see it in myself, but as the day went on a new me, the actual original me, was emerging. It slowly started to rise inside of me. And then I started crying for all the lost years that this beautiful me was buried under so much anger and hate and sadness. Something inside of me recognised this original person who then stood up inside of me. I feel so free and light and when you feel like this, you do not have any desire to yell and be angry anymore. And when you reach this state of mind, you can pass it on to others by seeing them for who they originally were before the alcohol and drugs and poverty. And maybe it would touch them in the same way."

Experiment: Reinvent yourself

Journal about the following questions:

- What did you do differently in the past year?
- What did you do for the first time in the past year?
- What did you stop doing in the past year?
- What new signs of life are you seeing that were not present in your life 12 months ago?
- What new passions are you becoming aware of?
- What sparkling event from earlier in your life have you started revisiting?
- Where did you shift from anxiety to passion?

I once facilitated a workshop, asking people to tell of a time that they reinvented themselves successfully in a small or big way.

During the feedback, one of the participants explained that he was shooting videos in Manenberg, a very poor area in Cape Town. He was gathering footage for a newspaper that wanted to report on gang violence and how the government has sent in the army to help fight the ongoing violence. Observing the environment, he saw the youngsters walking the streets with the typical swing of their hips. This way of walking, with its very specific rhythm, is characteristic of "skollies" or gangsters. And all of a sudden it reminded him that he used to walk like that when he was younger.

He continued to explain that at the age of 19 he had made a radical spiritual decision that changed his life. It was an inward decision that had many outward manifestations. "It changed the way I dressed, talked and eventually how I walked," he said.

The walking took a while. "I intuitively knew that I needed to change my walking as well. But I was ashamed of the fact that I could not change that immediately, so I decided to practise behind a closed door. To my surprise, the 'normal walk' appeared almost immediately and just stayed. Never again did I have to think consciously when I stood up in the morning, walking to the bathroom. It just happened organically."

He continued with a big open smile on his face, "This inner energy is like oxygen, it flames up immediately!" It was wonderful to revisit this energy within him. "Creating a new you can become a drug," he said.

"So yesterday, when I saw the gangster walk in action, I thought, that is the old me. I am different now. And I am different without trying to be different."

Another participant commented, "Imagine if you can revisit this energy every morning before your day starts!"

Ⓑ Reliable bearer of care

"A tree without roots is just a piece of wood."
– MARCO PIERRE WHITE

You may also be called from *without*. Here you are being pushed off balance, either by an assignment given to you or by an event that has forcibly destroyed your status quo and has shaken you. You are looking for a new equilibrium. Here it is important to be aware of your environment. What is calling you? Who is inviting you? Even if the call comes as a surprise or a disaster, it is ultimately a calling from Life (god/God).

The growth towards authenticity now depends on the nature of this challenge given to you.

In this scenario, Little Hans, our traveller, must choose between three goddesses. Each one of them represents a different value. So Little Hans is really being asked which value will lead his life. He is choosing his destiny.

Who you are when this call happens, signifies what the call is for you. "Where you were and what you were doing" when the call happened will determine the trajectory of your inner growth.

Your false inside can also be rigid, showing a fixed version of yourself. "You won't be able to change me." You cling to who you feel you have always been. This will not help you. The call from without helps you to answer a second core question: How can I fully embrace the reliable core of who I am and always have been?

This outer call invites you to focus on your strengths and gifts, and use these anew.

It could also be that everything in your life has just changed through a fateful event or disaster. Falling in love or discovering infidelity. Getting laid off or falling ill. All of these events can have the power to call us to reembrace our own reliable core.

When your sense of reality is challenged and you are being sent on a quest for meaning, "Who I think I am" must die. You must descend into the unknown. You must question the ideas you have about yourself.

Create a personal manifesto

The word manifesto comes from the Latin *manifestus* – to manifest, to clearly reveal, to make real.

A manifesto is a statement to declare your intentions, motives or beliefs.

A personal manifesto expresses your core values and beliefs. It reveals the specific ideas and priorities that you have always stood for, and how you plan to live your life going forward. This acts as both a statement of conviction and a call to action. A personal manifesto can help frame your life. It can help you to achieve your goals, and function as a tool to remind you of your key strengths and gifts. Start by asking yourself: What things have I always stood for? What are my strengths, gifts and beliefs? How do I want to live my life? How do I want to define myself? What words do I want to live by? Write these insights down as a personal manifesto.

Write your positive, uplifting manifesto by asking yourself questions like:

- What would personal clarity mean for me?
- How do I define myself? What do I stand for?
- According to what words do I want to live my life?
- What would social honesty mean for me?
- What are my strongest values and beliefs?
- What do I stand for?
- What would holistic grounding mean for me?
- How do I want to live my life?
- What changes will I make so that I can *live my best life*?

Write your manifesto in strong, positive language, short sentences, and in the present tense.

Write the manifesto to clarify what you believe and what type of contribution you want to make in this world.

C Radiate inner confidence

"Trust thyself: every heart vibrates to that iron string."
– RALPH WALDO EMMERSON

Lastly, you may be called from *below*. Sometimes this invitation to the quest is called the blunder. In a sense all calls to adventure are blunders. We never really know what we are getting ourselves into when we begin. If it is a true quest for authenticity, it always means we are getting in over our heads. For it is only when we get in over our heads that we are truly forced to change.

"A blunder is a mistake, but a significant one," Keith Cunningham said. Our blunders are always a call to wake up. This calling from below is an invitation to become more real, to face life.

Our disconnected false inside can be an attempt to be untouchable. It can be a way of hiding behind a wall. We smile, but in a detached way. We display a very modest attitude and can easily be ignored by others.

This calling from below can help you with the third question of the week: How can I be an abundant and content source of rest for everyone?

Recall the last time you made a significant mistake. It probably started with something very small.

Our friend Little Hans is on his way to a girl that fascinates him. In his infatuation, he forgets to secure one of his horses. And then it happens. He pulls on the rope and the horse slips loose. It all happens in slow motion. Just for a moment, his fascination with the girl knocks him off centre. He gets blinded by something innocent. And a whole new world unfolds before him. In the hero's journey, this is called an inciting incident. This is Little Hans's incident. It often happens when one loses focus for a split second. The consequences of that split second can change the course of the story.

A calling from below, to invite Freud, is the result of suppressed desires and conflict. From deep in your soul an opening to destiny opens up.

The quests asks of you to see what is blinding you. It invites you to turn around and look at your blind side. Often our extreme overdevelopment in one side of life makes us unable to see another side.

When you doubt yourself, it is difficult to see the new birth happening inside of you. But doubt creates space for new growth. And new birth is messy. It does not happen without pain and angst.

One day, I was facilitating a process with a group of managers. I can still see this well-groomed and hard-working middle manager with years of experience in a financial company sitting in front of me. She was telling me of a young new colleague in the company with an energy she envied. He brings excitement and joy that made her doubt herself. "I see other people behave with self-confidence. And I am jealous. I also want to be like that. But my self-doubt begins early morning in the shower. I am facing problems that I do not know how to handle. It is as if a little wheel starts to spin. And those days it just gets worse as the day continues. People listen to him."

The challenge is how to use this same energy to move from anxiety to passion.

Envy is a mirror of potential. We spot what we've got. We usually use the word projection to describe a negative trait. But you can also project the competency that is deep inside of you onto others. You see in others what you carry inside yourself, but sometimes you are too scared to embrace or show it.

These callings from within, without and below invite you to a journey of authenticity.

We have chosen Little Hans as a metaphor to help explain the hero's journey in more detail. Little Hans's real adventure actually begins this week. He receives a call to action. We don't know what it will be. It could be a direct threat to his safety or the comfort of his family, or it could be a disruption of his way of life or the peace in the community of which he forms part. It may be as dramatic as a gunshot, or simply a message or conversation. Whatever the call, and however it manifests, it ultimately disrupts the comfort of Little Hans's world and presents a quest that he must undertake.

Read the following 12 Laws of ME and try to see clearly how they could help you:

Reinvent yourself,
reclaim your reliable core, and
radiate inner confidence.

The 12 laws of ME

I only do what feels good.
I feel grateful for my place in life.
I know I am the only one not passing by.
Because I give love, I receive love.
I stay loyal to the ME I have become.
I facilitate my own strength.
I am the source of all my knowing.
I am exactly what others need from me.
I look forward with joy to everything that happens to me.
I know everybody wants to be of help.
I feel happy and I smile, always and everywhere.
I let my roots give me grounding.

My authentic inside

Read the following condensed description of your authentic inside. Become aware of how much of it is true for you at this moment. How much of it is a deep longing you have? What emotions are awakened by this description?

My deepest inside has a need to focus on being there for all that is needed. I am content and the source of rest for everyone, especially myself. I can be there for others from a fulfilled self.

I love, give safety and embrace from my abundance.

When I am really myself, I radiate inner confidence. I have an unwavering belief in life and its possibilities. I radiate safety and reassurance deep from within my heart. For me, nothing is too much trouble. There is no need to impress. My inside embodies inner strength turned into self-confidence.

Write down in your journal what happened to you while reading this description of your inside.

Task: Ask why questions

- If you think about your inner being often, ask yourself: Why do I find myself so important?

- If you almost never think about your inner being, ask yourself: Why am I not myself?

Getting to know yourself

People with a low awareness of their inside often do not know themselves. There are a number of ways in which we can start affirming and discovering our needs, wants and hopes.

Choose three of the following activities and complete them this week:

- Create a collage representing "The real me". You are allowed to use any materials you wish.
- Make a to-do list. Identify the three most important things and focus your efforts there, to start with. The to-do list can be about tasks in your life that need closure. The point of this exercise is to practise getting things done and celebrate your ability to do so.
- Practise saying affirmations or mantras. Make a list of five affirmations and keep them with you. Read them often. These are affirmations about your strengths.
- Make a list of short-term and long-term goals: What are the most important things for you to do today? This week? This month? And in the next three years?
- Describe an ideal scenario for a goal that you have.
- Write a poem expressing your feelings. It may be a poem about your feelings in general or your feelings about yourself.
- Reflect on: "What I value most in life".

Practise eye contact

It can be uncomfortable to truly look someone in the eye, but it is an essential part of being fully present in conversations. Maintaining eye contact will make the person you are speaking with feel validated. It also signals that you are proud and centred in yourself.

Holding someone's gaze during a conversation will make them feel they can trust you. However, it is okay to look away every once in a while, as staring intently without a break may make some people feel uncomfortable.

Reflection: Checking in on my inside

- How often did you manage to do your journaling?
- What light bulb moments did you have?
- Where in the week did you experience a special moment?
- What did you struggle with?
- Where are you starting to reinvent yourself?

"When there is no enemy within, the enemies from outside can do you no harm."

– AFRICAN PROVERB

For the more adventurous

- **Fairy tale** » Write and illustrate a fairy tale about yourself. If you could put yourself in a happily-ever-after situation, what role would you play and how would the story go? Create a book that tells the tale.

- **Unique snowflake** » Create a snowflake out of paper. Write ideas on the snowflake about the ways in which you are unique.

- **Mind mapping** » Make a visual representation of your thoughts to figure out how your mind works.

- **Family sculpture** » Create a family sculpture. For this activity, you can make a clay representation of each family member – mother, father, siblings, and any other close or influential family members – to explore emotional dynamics and roles within your family.

- **Fingerprint image** » Make art with your fingerprints. Your fingerprints are as unique as you are. Use ink and paint to create with your fingerprint images.

- **Blot-art** » Create blot-art. Here are the steps: Fold a piece of paper in half and open it again. Paint something abstract on the one side of the piece of paper – you can paint up to the crease. Fold the paper on the same crease while the paint is still wet. Open the page again while the paint is still wet. You will now see a mirrored abstract image. Like a classic Rorschach test, look at your image and describe what you see.

THREE
Recognising the full worth of my grounding

I am my own best friend.

Planning – the continuity of the now

This week we turn to being in the now. We nurture an inner compass that shows our direction in life. We face our feelings of unease and fears of not being grounded. We start to say goodbye to things that appear fixed in order to become more open to the here and now. We continuously practise peace of mind in the current situation. This leads to being comfortable with ourselves, filled with love for everything.

> *"Cease to inquire what the future has in store,*
> *and take as a gift whatever the day brings forth."*
> – HORACE

I am my own best friend.
I am open to the here and now.
I practise peace of mind.
I accept – it is what it is.

What to expect this week: Overcoming fears

Week 3 confronts you with your own resistance to change. You may become aware of your fear of the unknown. You may try different strategies to refuse this calling to your authentic self. The easiest route is to refuse to take any action, hoping your life will go back to "normal". But it will not.

It is also during this week that things and people in your environment will make light of your efforts to live authentically. Uncertainty and indecision will rear its head. As soon as you respond to the call to be yourself, the doubter, as Keith Cunningham calls it, appears on the scene. We recognise the doubter as the penetrating voice of secret anxiety: "Forget about that (her or him), you are not worth it. I mean, first you would have to cross the obstacle – and no one has ever done that. And then you would have to face this danger – and no one has ever done that. And if you finally, by some miracle, do arrive where you are going, what will you find? Another barrier. With the corpses of everyone who tried before you to conquer it. So forget about her, him or it. There is enough good stuff around you. Let me show you some ..."

This voice of doubt alone may be enough to stop you in your quest. As soon as you set your heart on reinventing yourself, anxiety comes along. You may fear the risks involved. There is the fear of not getting what you want, the fear of what you will have to sacrifice to get what you want, the fear of being cut off ... Your new quest automatically focuses on the fear. They are a pair of opposites. The external resistance is simply a concrete expression of the doubt you already feel inside.

Although Little Hans may be eager to accept the quest, at this stage he has fears to overcome. He is filled with second thoughts or even deep personal doubts as to whether he really is up to the challenge. This results in Little Hans refusing the call. The problem he faces may seem too much to handle and the comfort of home far more attractive than the dangerous road ahead. His refusal to start on his quest brings suffering.

What is happening to me?

I find this to be one of the most difficult directions of awareness to explore.

First, read through the first paragraph of this chapter and use the sentence that challenges you the most. For me, this sentence is: We nurture an inner compass that shows our direction in life.

I found myself wondering how one can distinguish between different anxieties.

How do you know which anxiety you are dealing with? Is this anxiety taking you to your old strategy? Or is this anxiety existing because you are moving through the mist in the forest using you inner compass towards your authentic self? Is this anxiety driving you forward or making you long for your old strategy?

To help myself, I drew two columns on a paper. On the right-hand side, I wrote down all the anxieties that came up while reading the sentence that stood out for me. For example, a workshop is being cancelled. Does that mean they do not like the work I am doing? And does that mean they (my corporate client) will cancel the rest of the workshops as well?

To complete the left-hand column, take a deep breath and ask this question to your inner compass: Is this true? Are you working with facts, or are your feelings based on your own assumptions? Does it trigger a split loyalty to yourself and others? In other words, does focusing on the facts also seem like you are betraying yourself because you are not taking your negative emotional response seriously?

If you shut out all the forces and anxieties (like the economy and the demands of others) in the environment for a moment, ask this question again in this state of mind: What direction do I need to take in order to be true to my inner compass?

When I pondered on these questions the following popped for me, prompting me to write on the left-hand side: "No, they are busy with bigger processes in the company. I need to pause and let them sort that out first. This is not about me."

I felt peace and quiet settle in me. But immediately the doubter asked, "Are you sure, or are you in denial and just trying to soothe yourself?"

If you experienced rest and peace for a moment, trust it and stick to it. A moment of peace is often the truth. Take your journal and do the following exercise with the sentences that stood out for you: Think about a person in your life who is peaceful about the future. What does this person model for you?

I recall the following that my mother once told me: "My doctor said one of the most beautiful things he has come across in his practice is the amount of peace and acceptance old people often have about their future."

My authentic grounding

My authentic grounding makes me naturally comfortable in myself and I am at peace.

I no longer focus on myself. I am connected to life and filled with love for everything.

My authentic grounding has an autonomy that distinguishes me from other people.

I am anchored and calm, radiating inner power. I am enough in myself and can be there for others without feeling threatened, exposed or judged. My authentic grounding seems unperturbed by the turmoil of life. It seems as if the turmoil of life only makes me stronger. I am an example for many but I am unlike most others. I do not let society, material wealth, greed or competition influence who I am.

Threshold guardian

Your quest is a journey to reach an important goal in life. But you will be travelling through an obstacle-strewn terrain. Each obstacle is typically patrolled by "guardians" with power. In stories these are called threshold guardians.

In movies we meet them as rival henchmen or lesser villains. Sometimes they may only be morally neutral figures. They could also be objects or elemental forces that are simply in your way.

These guardians represent the obstacles we encounter in life. We need to overcome barriers like bad luck, nasty weather, hostility, rejection and prejudice. At a deeper level, they also represent our inner demons. We need to face inner hindrances like emotional scars, vices and obsessions that manifest themselves strongly early in our quest.

Who or what is functioning as a threshold guardian in your life?

The main function of your specific threshold guardian is to test you. He, she or it is not necessarily evil in itself. Indeed, they may help you clearly understand and cross thresholds of resistance. The presence of such a guardian is also an indication that there is a possible boundary to cross.

At this stage of his journey our friend Little Hans has to solve a puzzle before the guardian will allow him to continue his journey, or he has to challenge the guardian, offer a bribe or sidestep him. The challenge this week is to learn to recognise threshold guardians, not necessarily as enemies but as opportunities to grow and acquire new power.

The way you will get around the people or things blocking your path will be specific to who you are. Use who you really are to figure out a way to get around the obstacles before you. This is why this journey focuses on identifying your strengths, as these strengths are your most useful tools on your journey.

When I did this journey for the first time, a lady contacted me out of the blue to do a project in a corporate environment. We met but did not have any natural chemistry. To my surprise she arranged another meeting with other role players in the organisation. Again, there was no natural flow in the meeting. Then it dawned on me that they were threshold guardians. I must not give up. Instead, I must persevere and learn what I need to learn to overcome the obstacles and resistance to transition into doing bigger projects. The insight helped me to not take the very direct critique to heart, but to see the bigger picture and the gift in the dynamics playing out. I ended up deciding that the way I usually do things – to provide all the services myself – might not be the way to go this time. I discovered that I could use other people to provide my services for the company. They might even add value to my product. These guardians showed me the threshold I was facing at the time:
I needed to get people to help me in order to increase my reach.

Ⓐ Certainty is an illusion – be open to the here and now

"One doesn't discover new lands without consenting to lose sight of the shore for a very long time."
– ANDRE GIDE

This week, you will be confronted with the question: How can I say goodbye to things that appear fixed in order to become more open to the here and now?

My false grounding can make me feel as if everything is uncertain and threatening. When this happens, I struggle to find the inner anchor I am searching for in the chaos surrounding me.

Question your assumptions.

We often use assumptions to help us make sense of the world quickly. This makes our world predictable. At least, that is how it feels to us. But this illusion of certainty can be wrong. Even when we understand that our assumptions can be incorrect, we tend to stick to them because they are familiar and comfortable.

What would happen if you start putting a question mark instead of a period after each of the ideas, opinions and viewpoints you are certain about? Could this help you engage in an argument with yourself on some of your thoughts and worldviews? Could this prevent you from falling prey to baseless convictions?

Worry collage

Create a collage of your worries. What worries you in your life? Cut out pictures from magazines to represent these worries, or maybe you want to draw something that scares you.

B Practising peace of mind

"If you cannot find peace within yourself, you will never find it anywhere else."

— MARVIN GAYE

At this stage you may feel tentative about this quest you have embarked on because it means change and hard work. Maybe you would like to stay in your comfort zone and decide what adventures you want to go on.

American author and businessman Seth Godin calls this the Icarus deception. He retells the legend of Icarus who died above the Icarian Sea just south of the Greek island of Samos. Daedalus, a master craftsman, fashioned a set of wings for himself and his son, Icarus, to escape from prison. Daedalus warned his son not to fly too close to the sun, but Icarus disobeyed. Icarus flew too high and the sun's heat caused the wax on his wings to melt. So he plunged into the sea and died. The lesson, we were told, is this: Don't disobey authority. Don't imagine that you are better than you are. Never believe you have the ability to do what only a god would be able to do.

However, there is a part of the myth that we were *not* told: Daedalus, in addition to telling his son Icarus not to fly too high, also instructed him not to fly too low because the water would weigh down his wings, ruining his ability to fly.

There is just as much danger in flying too low as there is in flying too high. Flying low might feel safe. So we settle for low expectations and small dreams. We aim for less than we are capable of. We are so obsessed about the risk of shining brightly that we avoid it at all costs.

But you are who you are. So take that path. Be human. Do the art. Fly higher than you were taught. Claiming the ground that has been given to you does not always feel safe. Your comfort zone feels safe. The secure job feels safe. The office feels safe. The familiar colleagues feel safe. However, you are holding yourself back by playing small.

"Our deepest fear is that we are powerful beyond measure. It is our light, not our darkness, that most frightens us. Your 'playing small' does not serve the world. There is nothing enlightened about shrinking so that other people won't feel insecure around you."
– MARIANNE WILLIAMSON

Being reluctant to the call

Your refusal to go on the quest is usually demonstrated by being afraid of what lies ahead. Therefore, you offer a load of excuses not to answer the call.

Your false grounding tries to block everything that makes you think of doing things "differently". You fear everything will collapse. You are watchful for potential danger.

List of excuses

Read through the following list of excuses. Make ticks next to those that you have expressed. Circle those that you secretly think about but do not verbalise.

Excuses about myself

This is not my job.
I don't have the time for that.
I don't have a mandate for that.
This is not my problem.
I don't like the idea.
You're right, but …
You can't teach an old dog new tricks.
Don't you think we should first look at the future before we act?
I know someone who has already tried that.
Let's sleep on it.
It cannot be done.
This is too much trouble.
That is impossible.
I've always done it that way.
Let's think about it a little more.

Excuses about others

It really is not our responsibility.
We are too busy to do this.
We don't have enough hands.
Our setup is too small for that.

People will never buy into it.

We are not ready for that yet.

The authorities will not approve it.

We did well without it.

That is all we can expect from the people.

The clients will not like it.

It won't work here with us.

What are they doing at other places?

People will laugh at us.

We've already tried that.

We've never done this before.

Excuses about my environment

Our circumstances are different ... more difficult.

This involves far-reaching change.

But the surroundings tell us ...

Let's do some proper research first.

The opposition will go crazy.

This is against our policy.

Let's get back to reality.

Don't fix something that is not broken.

You are two years ahead of your time.

We don't have the money, equipment, space or staff to do it.

It's not within the budget.

Let's just put it on hold for a bit.

First put it in writing.

In the long run this will cost us a lot of money.

Let's set up a think tank.

The challenge of this week is to answer the question: How can I continuously practise peace of mind in the current situation?

C Acceptance – it is what it is

"Life is such a gift, I just say thank you all day."

– NATALIE COLE

Alternatively, our false grounding could cause us to close our eyes, as if nothing can happen. We may choose to rather be on our own than facing threats by acknowledging our surroundings.

This week, we will help you to see change and uncertainty as a given and part of your plans. You can develop tolerance for failure and learn as you adjust to life. You are nurturing an autonomy that radiates inner power. You are busy answering the question: How can I be comfortable with myself, filled with love for everything?

Henri Nouwen calls his book *Reaching Out: The Three Movements of Spiritual Life* his "most personal thoughts and feelings". He describes the movement of reaching out to his innermost self. He calls this moving from loneliness to solitude. For him loneliness is one of the most universal human experiences, with society increasing the awareness of our loneliness. The roots of our loneliness are deep and cannot be touched by optimism or substitute love and social togetherness. This heightens our suspicion that there is no one out there who cares and loves us without conditions. We fear there is no place to be vulnerable without being used.

Read the following description by Henry Nouwen of our all-pervasive loneliness and journal about the feelings that surface in your mind and body (*Reaching Out*, p. 28).

> *It is this most basic human loneliness that threatens us and is so hard to face. Too often we will do anything possible to avoid the confrontation with the experience of being alone, and sometimes we are able to create the most ingenious devices to prevent ourselves from being reminded of this condition ... We have become so used to this state of anaesthesia, that we panic when there is nothing or nobody left to distract us. When we have no project to finish, no friend to visit, no book to read, no show to watch or no music to play, and when we are left all alone by ourselves we are brought so close to the revelation of our basic aloneness and are so afraid of experiencing an all-pervasive sense of loneliness that we will do anything to get busy again and continue the game which makes us believe everything is fine after all.*

Nouwen explains that if you wait for moments or places where no pain exists, where no separation is felt and where your human restlessness turns into inner peace, you are waiting for a dream world.

No friend or lover, no husband or wife, and no community or commune will ever be able to put to rest our deepest cravings for unity and wholeness.

Lindiwe (not her real name), a lawyer, moved from the northern part of South Africa to Cape Town in the south to put a distance of some 1500 kilometres between her and her ex-husband and to find peace of mind for herself and her children. However, in Cape Town she discovered utter loneliness. She felt isolated in this new environment, away from her family and friends. This fuelled anger towards her ex-husband. She felt even more miserable. During this time, she decided to read Henry Nouwen's book *Reaching Out*. Then it dawned on her that she was waiting for someone else, a different place or another job to bring inner peace. She realised that she has never been alone.

She started to use the loneliness as a gift to connect with herself. She gained insight into her life journey. She let go of the anger that was following her even before marrying her ex-husband. She embraced the change.

Weeks later, while driving to work, she noticed something for the first time. She discovered that she enjoyed the beautiful surroundings of the sea and Table Mountain. She reached out to new friends. She enjoyed a new-found deep happiness inside of her. She was able to talk to her children's father without irritation and anger. She could even reach out to him about the children's wellbeing.

The courage to enter the desert

What can we do with our essential aloneness? Nouwen explains we must enter the movement from loneliness to solitude. He suggests we must first find the courage to enter the desert of our loneliness and "to change it by gentle and persistent efforts into a garden of solitude". Here we go from outward-reaching cravings to inward-reaching search. We move from fearful clinging to fearless play.

However, solitude does not mean being alone by yourself in an isolated place. It is rather an inner quality or attitude. A sensitivity to listen to your inner voice. It is about maturing and slowly converting your loneliness into solitude. It is about being patient towards all that is unsolved in you and trying to love the questions themselves. Live the question.

Nouwen explains:

> Without the solitude of heart, the intimacy of friendship, marriage and community life cannot be creative. Without the solitude of heart, our relationships with others easily become needy and greedy, sticky and clinging, dependent and sentimental, exploitative and parasitic, because without the solitude of heart we cannot experience the other as different from ourselves but only as people who can be used for the fulfilment of our own, often hidden, needs.

Radiating inner power

Use the following meditation as a mantra (a repeatable slogan) for the week. Read it every day before journaling.

I am ...
Embracing my source
Accepting the now
Opening to change
Receiving the future
Sourcing wisdom
Embodying my roots
Becoming my being
Aligning with life
Consulting others
Connecting deeply
Being a gift
Showing myself.

Practising peace of mind

One of your main tasks for the week is to practise having peace of mind in your current situation – when you are alone. Read through the list of activities below and choose one or two that you can do on your own. No family, friends or pets – nothing. It is about you spending time with yourself.

- Sit in the sun and read something.
- Make yourself a healthy snack, choose a nice spot and enjoy it. Or cook your favourite meal, set the table nicely and eat by candlelight.
- Listen to music you love, or dance all by yourself.
- Go for a walk in a park, sit there for a while and watch the world go by.
- Go for a drive on a scenic route.
- Visit a museum or art gallery and browse leisurely.
- Find a spot on the beach or near water and eat a favourite snack.
- Wake up early and watch the sun rise from a good vantage point.
- Play! Think of roller skating, riding a bicycle or skipping rope. Go to a playground and swing on the swings.
- Rub fragrant lotion all over your body. Buy new perfume.
- Snuggle up under a cosy blanket and allow yourself to take that luxurious nap.
- Lie comfortably on the ground outside and watch the clouds go by. Notice the interesting shapes that might have meaning to you. Star gaze or daydream.
- Visualise your ideal future. What would it look like? Get a clear picture in your mind, write it down or create a vision board with what you see. Make a list of things you would like to do one day, even if they seem unattainable.
- Plan a vacation or staycation (be a tourist in your own city).
- Go on a retreat. Book out days for reflection and rest.
- Practise deep breathing.
- Spend time near, in or on water. Swim, float, wade or relax in a pool or at the beach.
- Do something you usually do but do this extra slowly today. Practise being present. Slow down and just allow yourself to be present.
- Practise relaxation techniques or relaxation therapy. Perform progressive muscle relaxation. Or try out a walking meditation in nature or in the city.
- Establish a tea ritual by gathering a variety of your favourite teas and additions. Use your favourite tea set and enjoy your tea.

Task: Ask why questions

- If you often think about *being comfortable in the now,* ask yourself: Why do I always like to know what I'm up against?
- If you almost never think about *being comfortable in the now,* ask yourself: Why can't I find peace in myself?

Reflection: Checking in on my grounding

- How often did you manage to do your journaling?
- What light bulb moments did you have?
- Where in the week did you experience a special moment?
- What did you struggle with?
- Where did you practise to be your own best friend?

For the more adventurous

- **Create a mandala »** Use a traditional sand box or draw your own mandala on paper. Create a drawing or painting using colours that you find calming.
- **Fleeting projects »** Sometimes we have a hard time letting go. This project will teach you that it is okay if something does not last. Use materials like sand, chalk, paper or water to create art that you can let go or discard afterwards.
- **Gratitude tree »** What are you grateful for? Write on leaves to create a gratitude tree. This project asks of you to write down those things on leaves to construct a tree or banner of gratitude.
- **Prayer flag »** Make a prayer flag. Send your prayers for yourself or those around you out into the universe with this flag.
- **Draw with closed eyes »** Draw with your eyes closed. Not being able to see what you are drawing intensifies fluidity, intuition, touch and sensitivity.
- **Body canvas »** Use your body as a canvas. You don't need paper when you have your body. Paint on your hands and feet or anywhere else to feel more in touch with yourself.

FOUR
Recognising the full worth of my friendship

I am surrounded by people that love me, and vice versa.

Connection – the bonding I experience

This week, you will explore another aspect of your roots, namely connection. You will explore the feelings in your heart when you are around others. You will identify how you experience bonding with others, and your fear of not being loved or not getting into a relationship. You will look at how you try to convince people to like you, as well as how to establish a social environment that serves everyone. In that way you can learn to be there for others, no matter who they are, making everyone feel at ease.

"I think relationships are work, but love is a gift."
– ANNE HATHAWAY

I am surrounded by people who love me, and vice versa.

I don't let friends do silly things – alone.

I am a relationship builder.

I accept without reserve.

What to expect this week: Meeting your mentor

In week 4, you will work with overcoming your fear of searching for and finding who you really are. Be on the lookout for a mentor or new community that will support you on this journey.

At this crucial turning point where Little Hans desperately needs guidance, he meets a mentor figure. This person gives him something he needs. He could be given an object of great importance. Or he may receive insight into the dilemma he faces. It could be wise advice or practical training. Sometimes it is just self-confidence. Whatever the mentor gives to Little Hans, it serves to dispel his doubts and fears. It gives him the strength and courage to continue his quest.

Your guide will often appear in your life out of nowhere. At first it may not be obvious to you who your guide is.

Think about the people who are in your life at this stage:

- Is there anyone who has joined your "circle"?
- Is there anyone who is new to your world?
- Does anyone make you feel uncomfortable?
- Does anyone challenge how you think about life?
- Did anyone invite you to join them on an unpredictable "project"?

The saying goes, "When the student is ready the teacher appears." The truth is that the student is never ready. This week you will encounter people ready to instruct you. These guides live in your authentic world. They are part of you non-ego world, and they will accompany you in the remaking process of your life. Your job is to recognise them.

Remember, your guide or mentor is a close ally. She or he will train and guide you during the pursuit of your goal.

While a guide is sometimes someone in your life, she or he could also remind you of something deep inside of you. The inner take on this is that she or he presents your higher self. She or he reminds you of the wiser, nobler and more god-like aspects of yourself.

What will your guide be doing at this stage of your journey? Through teaching and training, she or he is preparing you for the challenges ahead.

This is often a two-way process. Your mentor will also be learning from you.

Often mentors help you attain your goal by giving a gift, be it a "weapon", a cure, a symbol or other ways to survive. This gift is often given to you after you have made a self-sacrifice or a commitment. All of this provides you with inspiration, direction and incentive.

But beware, guides and mentors are shadowy and shifty. They are not easily pinned down. They do not play by the rules and they live close to the world of instinct. Guides know much more than you because they have already been on this journey. They have returned to help you. Your guide does not need a social persona and will not be wearing a social mask. She or he does not "play by the rules" of society.

Your guide will not represent the "daytime" values of your society. However, she or he is the "human form" of your new future. And maybe, just maybe, your guide is someone who steers you to search inside yourself for the guiding principles for your journey.

Journal on the following questions

- What shadowy parts of the guides that are appearing in your life are you recognising in yourself?
- What parts of the guides' higher values do you know are also part of you?

Recognise the shift

Make a list of all the shifts that are happening in your life. Also list the shifts happening to the people and in the environment around you.

My authentic friendship

Out of my authentic friendship I am always willing to be there for others, no matter who they are. I am trusting and kind, open and welcoming, making everyone feel at ease immediately.

My authentic friendship, per definition, has the ability to see the goodness in people. Everyone immediately feels at ease around me.

This means that people deeply know they are welcome; people are seen for who they are and not (only) for what they do. My authentic friendship is hospitality personified. I facilitate peace in the group and reduce tension. I ensure that people start talking to each other again.

A Don't let friends do silly things – alone

"People will forget what you said. They will forget what you did. But they will never forget how you made them feel."

– MAYA ANGELOU

The first question you will be pondering this week is: How can I steer everyone to get them to like me?

In our world, says Henry Nouwen, the assumption is that strangers are a potential danger and that it is up to them to disprove it. This does not lead to authentic living. The Afrikaans word for hospitality is "gasvryheid". It means freedom for the guest. We find true connection when we create free spaces for others.

Active connecting

The first level of connecting is a little bit like dating.

I was 32 years old and single, independent and living in my own house near the sea. I had a good job, was part of a supportive circle of friends and very connected with my extended family. Most weekends I had family and friends over and people enjoyed spending time at my place.

I wish I could say that I was happily enjoying life on my own. But no, there was this nagging feeling of loneliness. At the same time I was starting to make peace with the fact that I would stay in this "independent" state for the rest of my life. When sadness came to visit me, I picked myself up, reminding myself of all the good things in my life.

Then one day in a bookshop this book caught my eye: *If I am so wonderful, why am I still single?* I made sure no one saw me buying it and sneaked out of the shop. It was not the best book I have ever read, but the message I received was this: Put yourself actively out there ... get yourself to places to meet people. Ask people to introduce you to people ... tell the universe you are available. You haven't settled for this.

My anxiety went through the roof. I was settled in my circle of friends. We had a kind of routine over weekends. I was the one in my family who was always available. I could not do this. I would focus more on my work and part-time studies. There would enough things to keep me busy.

Then, out of the blue, it happened while I was busy doing my chores. I had to plan a family camp as coordinator of the wellness programme at a nuclear power station near Cape Town. The last time I camped was as a student together with other people from my church. My brother was involved in a student community, doing the one camp after the other. So I phoned him. Very early in the conversation, he referred me to a student doing his master's degree and working part-time for the community. "He is the expert in camping and developing programmes. I think you need to contact him to help you." My brother's wife commented in the background, "You never know! He is such a nice guy."

Immediately my anxiety flared up. I just wanted to do my work properly ... and now this! Do I contact him? Would he want to see me? How do I go about this? So I just called him.

On the other side, a young voice answered. Very polite, but also very determined not to talk to me. He had a few handouts with ideas and he would drop these at my brother's place.

Susan Page's book *If I am so wonderful, why am I still single?* motivated me just enough to make me say the following sentence that would change the course of my life, "I am coming to Stellenbosch on Friday anyway. Where can we meet?" (Today, he is my husband.)

My false friendship is sometimes not sure what people are thinking of me. I then feel uncomfortable in groups and choose to stay only with people with whom I feel safe. When this happens, people can experience me as forceful or challenging, even exclusive or overbearing.

Unplugging

Connecting with people and putting away your electronic devices before any conversation signify that you are giving your full and undivided attention to the other person.

If your phone or laptop demands your attention, let it go. Remain present and focused on what the other person is saying.

Connect human being to human being.

Human interaction is underpinned by universal needs such as respect, competence, social status and autonomy. When you recognise these deeper needs it kindles trust and positive behaviour. Paul Santagata, Head of Industry at Google, likes to challenge teams to remember that the other party is just like them. He leads them through a reflection called "Just like me", which asks them to consider the following:

- This person has beliefs, perspectives and opinions, just like me.
- This person has hopes, anxieties and vulnerabilities, just like me.
- This person has friends, family and perhaps children who love them, just like me.
- This person wants to feel respected, appreciated and competent, just like me.
- This person wishes for peace, joy and happiness, just like me.

How would it change your relationships and connections if you consider this to be true of the people in your life that you are shutting out, ignoring or fighting with?

B Be a relationship builder

"That was my mother's policy: Feel free, feel welcome. Be happy."

— BRIDGETT M. DAVIS

Your second question for the week is: What can I do to establish a social environment that serves everyone?

Often this starts by inviting friends over or creating a pleasant work environment where everyone feels connected and wanted.

The other day we were visiting friends when one said, "When we try to throw a party, we can never get it to be the party we've imagined! It feels boring with not enough zest to call it a party."

This reminded me of all our trial-and-error parties through the years. We have tried the big table sit-down dinner only to have a flat outcome. Before I knew it I was facilitating conversations and the poor guests became members of a "team building" without signing up for it.

Afterwards we decided that we worked way too hard, also during the evening, with no energy left to get the party going. One or both of us were in the kitchen the whole evening.

Whenever we want to create connection we remember our early lessens. For us, six to eight is the perfect number of guests. Or else we invite 12 or more people so that they can form their own little groups. We provide small social spaces for this to happen.

Do what you do best, whether it is a braai (a South African barbeque) or a simple meal with soup and bread, or coffee and cake. Or do what is locally done best. We stayed in a guest house for our first wedding anniversary and enjoyed a wonderful breakfast with freshly baked bread and muffins. When we complimented the owner she said, "Thank you, it is locally baked".

Since then we have decided to use our local resources to add to our tried-and-tested meals, and to keep it simple.

Create your kind of community and invite people accordingly. Take into consideration who you want to include.

Set the scene for connection. Coffee, snacks, calm music and enough chairs say "We want to talk, eat and connect". Loud music, no chairs, plates of snacks and lots to drinks say, "Eat, drink, dance and party the night away!"

Invite people with whom you have a connection, or people you would like to know better.

Connection starts with a hearty invitation.

Mutual understanding and vulnerability

Working with a group of IT people, I met David, a tall, shy but very respectful guy, working as a scrum master in an agile tech environment. He was the first scrum master I had met. Before him I did not know this term in the software development context. I discovered that the term was actually derived from rugby, the sport that inspired the IT thinkers to come up with this new way of working in teams.

At David's work we did a team intervention on awareness. It was supposed to support this new way of working. He was respectful and supportive. However, I could never tell whether what we were trying to do was actually assisting him in his job of managing different teams.

I was humbled when we met again a year later. He had wisdom that would help me a great deal on how teams are supposed to collaborate.

"It's all about trust, about team members trusting each other. Deep trust helps them moving forward with how they work and it increases productivity."

"Because of the mutual understanding and vulnerability, they seemed happier. They are more open about their thoughts. And that's what teams need."

Then he explained, "If you can reach a high level of trust in the team, you get softer, more introverted, more aware and consensus dialogue. Not just individual opinions."

Establish a social environment

The following tips can help you establish a social environment that serves the people around you. Read through the list and choose three things you want to start doing.

- Ask for feedback from people who have "less" power than you or who serve you.
- Admit your mistakes.
- Be open to opinions that differ from your own.
- Be welcoming and encourage people to ask you questions.
- Engage in active listening.
- Put away your phone during conversations.
- Show understanding by repeating what was said.
- Encourage people to share more by asking open questions. Don't try to "one up" people through your questions.
- Actively ask individuals who rarely speak during engagements for their opinions.
- Do not interrupt other people.
- When brainstorming or sharing, accept all ideas equally and do not judge.
- Never blame. Focus on solving the problem.
- Encourage out-of-the-box suggestions.
- Develop an open mindset. Approach situations from different angles.
- Encourage people to share feedback with one another.
- Encourage people to see feedback as a way to strengthen and build upon their ideas and processes.

This type of behaviour creates what Harvard Business School professor Amy Edmondson calls "psychological safety". Psychological safety is a shared belief that the group you belong to is safe for interpersonal risk taking. People are able to show and be themselves without the fear of negative consequences in the group. In this type of group culture we all feel accepted and respected.

Edmondson showed that psychological safety plays an important role in effectiveness. It improves the likelihood that an attempted process innovation will be successful. It also enables people to learn more from their mistakes, and it boosts engagement between people. It facilitates and improves innovation. We can then have respectful face-to-face conversations.

Our false friendship can make it difficult to let go of the familiar. When we are inflexible we often seek out the safe and recognisable group. We tend to operate with the picture of an ideal group in mind, without adjusting to the present group.

Create connection

We all have a deep longing for significant connection but often think that it will happen on its own. Choose one of ideas below (or think of one yourself). Write it down in your diary and make an appointment or, even better, stop reading and do it immediately:

- Set aside time to meet a friend, or plan and schedule a special date night with someone.
- Attend a caring support group.
- Volunteer and help someone else.

- Spend time with kids.
- Meet up with a long-lost friend or loved one.
- Bake something and invite someone over.
- Laugh.
- Ask someone to mentor you. Share your inner dialogue.
- Call or write a letter to someone you have lost touch with.
- Visit an elderly friend or relative and listen to their stories and wisdom.
- Hug someone, or ask for a hug. Ask a special person to nurture you (feed, cuddle or read to you).
- Write thank you notes. Write a letter to an old friend.
- Practise the art of forgiveness.
- Bake cookies or make something with your hands and give it away with an appreciative note.
- Take a break from technology. Spend time alone and enjoy the silence, or spend the time really connecting and communicating with the people you care about.
- Phone a friend or family member and tell them what is happening in your life. Just reconnect with someone you care about.

C Accept without reserve

"Love is always bestowed as a gift – freely, willingly and without expectation. We don't love to be loved; we love to love."

– LEO BUSCAGLIA

Our disconnected false friendship may hide behind slight grins. Then we are cautious about who comes close to us. Sometimes we make no real contact and are there without being there.

Spend time thinking about this question: How can I be there for others, no matter who they are, and help everyone feel at ease?

In *The Different Drum: Community Making and Peace*, M Scott Peck explains how he guided people into community. In the beginning, people deny the individual differences and try to create cheap community. This attempt to find community through shortcuts uses little white lies, withholding truths and feelings to avoid conflict and pretence. After the pretence, the group enters chaos and fighting. But this is also not true community.

True community comes through emptiness. For true community we need to empty ourselves of barriers to community. Our feelings, assumptions, ideas and motives make us as impenetrable as a billiard ball.

Deep connection is an adventure into the unknown. Rather than trying to force the experience and contact with others confirm your expectations. Stop trying to fit others and your relationship with them into a preconceived mould. Be open to really listen, hear and experience. Suspend your judgement of people, often built on very brief, limited experiences. Let go of your need to heal, convert, fix or solve. Rather start to appreciate and celebrate interpersonal differences.

True connection starts after we let go of our need to control. Life, and relationships, is not a problem to solve, but a mystery to embrace. There is no other way into true connection than through emptiness. And, there is no other way into connection than through sharing brokenness. Accepting without any reservations starts with myself. I embrace my defeats, my failures, my doubts, my fears, my inadequacies and my sins. I stop acting as if I have it all together.

However, it is not easy when you show your weaknesses and when others try to change you. It takes courage to confess vulnerability when others behave as if you have not said anything.

But when you have an awareness of accepting without reservation, you encourage the sharing of brokenness. You don't block expressions of pain and suffering. You now choose to embrace not only the light of life but also life's darkness. True connection is joyful, but also realistic.

Deep connection is a testament to the human spirit. When you are completely empty and open, you enter community. You experience a soft quietness. You are bathed in peace. You are speaking from the deepest part of yourself. You are comfortable in the silent hush that hangs between you and others.

Deep connection is lively and intense, but not easy. The agony is actually greater, but so is the joy. Even if there are times of anxiety, frustration and fatigue the dominant feeling is joy.

My connection commitment

I will listen deeply and not try to heal and fix.

I will seek the "argument" behind the words and not stick my own interpretation onto it.

I will validate and not criticise.

I will celebrate and not give advice.

Empathy

Empathy shows that you care and are willing to express compassion. When we put in the effort to understand how other people feel, it helps us to engage with them. This understanding will help us to respond appropriately towards others and to behave in a more supporting way.

You can acknowledge other people's emotions by trying to reflect the person's feelings accurately. Listen for key emotions and paraphrase what you have heard.

Express gratitude and appreciation

You could feel awkward expressing appreciation and gratitude in the workplace. However, doing this fosters an upbeat work environment.

Expressing gratitude and appreciation towards people creates a pro-social climate. Think of ways to express gratefulness, appreciation, recognition and acknowledgment towards colleagues and friends.

Task: Ask why questions

- If you often think about *your experience of bonding with others,* ask yourself: Why do I want everyone to like me?
- If you almost never think about *your experience of bonding with others,* ask yourself: Why do I struggle to make real contact with people?

Reflection: Checking in on my friendship

- How often did you manage to do your journaling?
- What light bulb moments did you have?
- Where in the week did you experience a special moment?
- What did you struggle with?
- Where could you clearly see integration between this journey and your life journey? Did you experience any synchronicity (the feeling that there is a reason why events that have no obvious connection are occurring at the same time)?

For the more adventurous

- **Anchor art »** Make anchor art. Who are the anchors in your life? In this project, you will make an anchor and decorate it with the people and things that provide you with stability and strength.
- **Build a home »** Build a "home". What does "home" mean to you? During this activity you will create a safe, warm place that feels like home to you.
- **Stuffed animal »** Soft, cuddly objects can be very comforting. Use this project to create an animal from your intuitive drawings. Work on a softness project. Using only soft or comforting objects, create a work of art.
- **Safe space »** Draw a place where you feel safe. This is an art therapy directive to find your safe place for healing from trauma.

STAGE 2

Twist
your trunk

The next four weeks will strengthen your trunk.

Your trunk awareness empowers and structures you. You experience power that directs your life and structures your being. Here you become aware of the consistency of your outer and inner life patterns.

> *"I was always looking outside myself for strength and confidence but it comes from within. It is there all the time."*
>
> – ANNA FREUD

FIVE
Recognising the full worth of my contribution

I know that I am a gift to my environment.

Relevance – the way I see my gift accepted

This week, we will take a look at your ambivalent feelings about your gift to others. Maybe you are unsure because you do not know what people need from you. Or you could be anxious about not being accepted. You are exploring your relevance; the way you see your gift being accepted. We will look at the ways in which you try to convince others that you know best what they need. You will be asked to optimise your chances of success by listening well and delivering precisely what others want. The reassuring part is giving yourself to others in order to focus on mutual fulfilment.

> *"Like a simple little lighthouse, my true ideal is to just be … having no trace of seeking, desiring, imitating, or striving, only light and peace."*
>
> – BODHI SMITH

I know that I am a gift to my environment.

I seek relevance.

I go for quality not hype.

I just stand and shine.

What to expect this week: Crossing a threshold

This is the week of commitment. You will set processes in motion that will make it impossible to turn back. You will cross a threshold with no option of turning back. You will never be the same again.

On this journey you are rewriting your story. This week, you will have to answer the call. Will you commit to the goal of living authentically? The beginning of your journey has ended; now your real journey begins. There is no turning back. Will you embrace the full range of awareness available to you?

Little Hans is now ready to act upon his call to adventure. He now truly departs on his quest. This can be a physical, spiritual or emotional quest. He may go willingly, or he may be pushed. Either way, Little Hans finally crosses the gateway between the world he is familiar with and the world of the unknown. Maybe he is leaving home for the first time in his life. Maybe he will do something he has always been too scared to do. The entry point will present itself. What Little Hans does with this, signifies his commitment to his journey and whatever it may have in store for him.

My authentic contribution

When I embrace my authentic contribution I give myself to others. I truly trust that "what comes from the heart" will always be welcome. Meeting others is about fulfilment and not filling a need.

I have an almost unnoticed presence and I am effective in achieving what is needed. My authentic contribution often retreats to the background, but my presence and love are always felt. I take care of what people want, even before they have voiced their needs. Without demanding attention and without effort, I unobtrusively add value to the people around me.

A Relevance is a bitch

> "Find out what your gift is and nurture it."
> – KATY PERRY

The first question to guide you this week is: How can I convince others I know best what they need?

Your false contribution does not take "the individual behind the person" into account. When you are making a false contribution, you are operating without seeing others. They might see your "pressing through" as efficiency.

In The Four Agreements: A Practical Guide to Personal Freedom, Don Miguel Ruiz invites us to make agreements with ourselves. In these agreements you will tell yourself who you are, what you feel, what you believe and how to behave. The fourth agreement he proposes is this: Don't make assumptions.

He explains that we have a tendency to make assumptions about everything. The problem with assumptions is that we, over time, start to believe that these assumptions are true. We decide what others are doing and thinking. We make assumptions, we misunderstand and end up creating a big drama about nothing.

Communicate rather than make assumptions.

Have the courage to ask rather than make assumptions.

Stop guessing what others want and need by making assumptions.

Ask how others feel rather than make assumptions.

Be quiet

This week, practise your ability to allow someone else to speak without any interruption. Use conversations as a time to be quiet. Focus on what the person is saying, and try to truly understand the message they are trying to convey.

We often have a tendency to make assumptions when we are missing a piece of information. Instead of asking questions when we do not know something, we jump to conclusions. Then we are speaking for others by projecting our own experiences onto them.

The best thing you can do is to ask additional clarifying questions. Engage in active listening by paraphrasing what the other person is saying: "This is what I hear you are saying. Is that correct?" Also ask factual questions that have not been addressed.

The soup pot grabber

I once was in a small boardroom of a promising new tech company. I was leading my very first team session with this new tool on awareness. The participants were the senior team of the IT development shop of one of the big brands in the financial industry. They shortened the session from half a day to two hours.

I put on my brave and friendly face, and explained as well as I could what every awareness archetype meant. They had to identify theirs (based on the assessment they did beforehand) and share it in pairs. The room started buzzing with people sharing. A few asked me to come over and clarify some things.

Shortly after asking the participants to share their insights in small groups, one guy shouted, "I'm a seller!" He was clearly ecstatic about this discovery. I went over to him to give the other participants time to finish their sharing. He could clearly not wait any longer. He was so impressed with his discovery that he wanted everyone in the room to know about it. He immediately got the meaning of the awareness archetypes.

The "seller" explained: "I was the youngest of five children. My mother was a magistrate. We often had intellectual debates at the dinner table. Because I was the youngest, I could rarely compete with the rest of the people around the table. By the time I had something to say, the game was over. I often left the table without saying a word."

He continued, "So one day, we were again sitting around the table having a heated debate. I actively tried to figure out how to make an entrance in this debate when I heard a splattering noise from the kitchen. Immediately I knew: The soup was boiling over and there would soon be a mess in the kitchen. I also immediately clicked this would be my chance of a lifetime. So I rushed to the kitchen and, with my bare hands, grabbed the pot of boiling soup from the hot stove and dumped it in the sink.

"By that time, the rest of my family were also standing in the kitchen. They were astonished by my brave act to save the family's meal despite the blisters already forming on the inside of my hands. I still remember that the satisfaction growing in my heart outweighed the physical pain I felt. I said to myself, I did it! I got their attention. I was first, not last. I heard something they did not and then did the right thing first!"

There I was standing in the room, again astonished by his quick reaction. He later told me in private that he often received negative feedback about this "attention-seeking" behaviour. (I thought of how he shouted out his discovery during the training session.) He started doubting himself, not because of the knowledge "coming" to him in an instant but because he knew that people did not always like him for this. He did not know whether he needed to keep quiet or to say something. As this was his big gift in life, he felt like nothing without it. At the same time, he felt that his gift was not accepted in a group.

Later, this man discovered that when he builds relationships with people, they would hear him and appreciate his gift. "It is only when I started drinking coffee with the guys for the sake of being and bonding that they started hearing me when we brainstormed. And it was then that I could start loving my 'seller' again for the gift it brings. I was no longer the 'youngest soup pot grabber' but an equal partner in this circle."

Months later, working at a new company, he told me, "I've stopped feeling I have to perform to be valuable. I am allowed to exist in this place."

Starting blocks

These starting blocks will help you to come up with initiatives and novel suggestions to start listening deeper.

Put on new shoes » Create an outline of someone who needs your contribution. This character may help to focus your creativity and ensure that you stay user-friendly. It is a good way to put yourself in another person's shoes.

Listen to outsiders » Collect the opinions of other people. Bring in people from other areas or offices, or talk to your clients.

Mingle » Eat lunch with a different person each day. Ask three people how they would improve your idea. Ask for help when you need it. Ask someone to collaborate with you on your favourite project.

Get fast feedback » Talk to people you trust. Ask for help. Schedule time with the smartest people at work. Visit your regulars more often. Find a mentor.

B Not hype but quality

"I like to listen. I have learned a great deal from listening carefully. Most people never listen."

– ERNEST HEMINGWAY

Your second question for the week is: How can I optimise my chances of success by listening well and delivering precisely what others want?

Your false contribution does what it always does, namely thinking that everyone should be satisfied with this. Then you try to convince people by telling stories of how others find what you do very helpful.

Remember David, the scrum master? This is how he described his inner journey regarding relevance.

"Earlier, I just wanted to dive in and start doing what I normally, naturally do. I did not want to take the time to sit back and say, 'Well, what is the expectation? Okay, how do I meet that?' And then ensure that we are all on the same page. That may be a more cautious approach but it helped me to really understand what they needed. Then I would go and put tick boxes next to what they needed in order to ensure I'm doing exactly that. Not just doing what I think they need or what I want to be. So it's a bit of a change.

"The other day I discovered that I have learned a new habit organically. Every morning, I slow down and ask: Okay, what are the expectations? What do I need to do? What do I need to check? I then do this during the day, ensuring that I'm doing what others are requiring – whether that is making the team happy, ensuring the team understands the scope of the work, or reporting back on progress. Whatever it is, I make sure that I'm going through all the steps to provide what they clearly said they require. It is more of a planned approach. Should I say I never used to do that?

"Somehow, this makes me really happy – that I address what people really need. They trust that I will do that; they trust each other to do the same. In this way, we are much more focused and aligned to deliver and be happy."

Relevance-centred awareness

Your environment and the people in it have needs. Which combination of the following questions can you ask people around you to get feedback? The answers to which questions will help you deliver precisely what they want?

1. **Information:** How can we increase our communication with you?
2. **Ease:** What would make it easier for you to meet your needs? How can we help?
3. **Clarity:** What would make it easier for you to work with me or be with me?
4. **Flow:** How could working or being with me be made more intuitive?
5. **Consistency:** What do I need to do so that you will get the same benefits each time I help you?

6. **Warmth:** What would communicate empathy and understanding to you?
7. **Openness:** What would make our relationship more transparent?

Additional questions for business settings

1. **Empowerment:** How can I give you more control in our interaction from start to finish?
2. **Choice:** What can I do to increase your freedom of choice?
3. **Price:** In what price range must I function so you will buy from me?
4. **Fairness:** What negotiated agreements would feel fair to you?
5. **Fit:** How can the things I do be made more compatible with what you are already doing?
6. **Efficiency:** How can we streamline your most time-consuming processes?
7. **Function:** What must my service or product do to solve your problem or desire?

Second-guessing people's experience of the relevance of your contribution can leave you in the dark. It is like singing in the shower – you enjoy it but you only hear your own voice. Asking people could be very insightful. It can help you to make your contribution more relevant and user-friendly.

It is fairly simple to find out how to please people – ask them.

C Lighthouses just stand there and shine

"People give one another things that can't be gift-wrapped."

– NADINE GORDIMER

The last question of the week is: How can I give myself to others in order to focus on mutual fulfilment?

Read through the following relevance mantras (repeatable slogans). Choose one to put up somewhere to focus on for the whole week.

- I step into the story and invite others in.
- I create hubs for the voices of citizens.
- I innovate towards meaning.
- I start from a human need.
- I shine a light on people already succeeding.
- I shorten the feedback loop.
- I pay attention to where I am now.
- I believe in here.
- I remember relevance to the customer or client.
- I seek solutions in cooperation.
- I build creative communities.

Our false contribution easily overlooks the wishes of others because we are filled with the blind faith that people will want what we offer.

Ask trusted friends for feedback.

To increase your awareness, ask people you trust for feedback. People who know you best can provide a mirror, be it positive or negative, on different aspects of your life. This could be about who you are, your interaction with other people or life in general. This may provide a perspective on yourself that you would otherwise never have noticed.

Ask a friend to highlight what your gifts are in a group when you are just being yourself.

Task: Ask why questions

- If you often think about *your gift to others,* ask yourself: Why do I want to be important to others?
- If you almost never think about *your gift to others,* ask yourself: Why don't I know what others want from me?

Reflection: Checking in on my contribution

- How often did you manage to do your journaling?
- What light bulb moments did you have?
- Where in the week did you experience a special moment?
- What did you struggle with?
- What are you discovering about your authentic contribution?

For the more adventurous

- **Gratitude object »** Choose the people who matter the most to you in life and create a unique artwork for each of them. This is a great way to acknowledge what really matters to you and to express your gratitude.

- **Good traits presentation »** Draw images or make a list of your good traits. Creating drawings or listing your positive traits will help you to become more positive and build a better self-image.

- **Hand plaster »** Sculpt your hand in plaster. Once it is dry, write all the good things you can do with it onto the hand. Think of ways you could add to the well-being of others.

- **Line art »** Lines are one of the simplest and most basic elements of art. Yet, they can also contain a lot of emotions. Use simple line art to demonstrate what difference you can make in the world.

SIX
Recognising the full worth of my creativity

I trust my own inspiration.

Knowledge – the greater source from which I tap

This week, we focus on the greater source of knowledge into which we tap. What do you do with the "light bulbs" of everything one could know? Does it make you anxious to not know or not feel your own wisdom? Sometimes, you need to think in a totally different way, or rethink what you have come to know as the truth. The promise is that you can trust that you will find the right knowledge when you need it.

"Happy people produce. Bored people consume."
– STEPHEN RICHARDS

I trust my own inspiration.
Truth and knowledge are within me.
I stand on the wisdom of many generations.
I am open to my inner source of knowledge.

What to expect this week: Obstacles and tests

In week 6 you experiment with living your authentic self. You have a new awareness of life and start living inside this new reality. You start building support structures. The obstacles and tests will be very real. Some of them will be emotional, others physical. You are invited to engage with your environment. Sometimes it will be fun and games; other times it will lead to resistance and struggle.

This week the energy of your quest will shift. You will discover new information that will make you more determined to commit to this quest for living authentically. This information can come from the inside or the outside, and it may be positive or negative.

Be on the lookout for a moment of grace, a moment of enlightenment or a mind-f*ck moment.

Little Hans is now way out of his comfort zone. He is confronted with an even more difficult series of challenges that test him in various ways. Obstacles are strewn across his path. These may be physical hurdles or people bent on preventing his progress. Little Hans must overcome each challenge with which he is presented on the journey towards his ultimate goal.

Little Hans needs to find out who can be trusted and who can't. He may win allies and meet enemies who will, each in their own way, help prepare him for the greater tests yet to come. This is the stage where his skills and powers are tested. Every obstacle that he faces helps us gain a deeper insight into his character.

During this week you will become aware of your new-found allies. You are gathering the knowing of many generations as preparation for your big challenge. You are getting close to reaching your goal. You need all the resources you have to prepare yourself for the upcoming challenge.

My authentic creativity

My authentic creativity trusts and then receives all that I need. I really believe in the power of letting go.

I know what needs to be known at exactly the right time I need to know it. My authentic creativity is open to receive this knowledge.

It seems that I recite from the work of others, but with a uniqueness and obviousness that speaks of my own deeper wisdom. I have access to my inner source of knowing. This source is aligned with the eternal source of knowing – even when the things I know seem separate from my knowledge and experience of the worldly reality. Through my knowledge, I serve more than my own affairs.

A Truth and knowledge is within me

"I think, at a child's birth, if a mother could ask a fairy godmother to endow it with the most useful gift, that gift should be curiosity."

– ELEANOR ROOSEVELT

How can we think totally different?

Our false creativity can be anxiously looking to find itself in what we create. Over and over again we think we are what we create. We associate our worth with what we produce. We can be persistent and unyielding. We may become very frustrated because we are afraid to be complacent. We feel as if we need to prove and renegotiate the whole time.

We create for the experience of being alive

We are called upon to design the world, not to fix the typos. It is easy to edit and criticise; however, the magic starts with initiating and creating.

Read through the following innovative mantras (repeatable slogans). Choose one to put up somewhere where you will see it for the whole week.

- I ground myself and think about what is possible.
- I work from primary evidence.
- I search for a touch of magic.
- I learn by doing.
- I frame the question strategically.
- I see what I've never seen before.
- I am inspired with other ideas.
- I become iconic by making a difference.
- I stop looking for trends and rather have an opinion.
- I lead people to do great jobs.
- I am simple and unpredictable.
- I joyfully embrace the crazy ones.
- I have something to say.
- I focus on good, not different.
- I stop talking about the future and start creating.
- I foster serious play at work.
- I celebrate imperfections.
- I use stories to imagine the impossible.

Starting blocks for innovation

Sometimes you just know that you need to come up with fresh and innovative ideas.

Think of a problem you are grappling with. Get the frustrations, problems and blockers clear in your mind's eye.

Read through the following list of starting blocks to jumpstart your creativity. Take a clean page and start writing, doodling or drawing new insights about the challenges in your life.

Which one of the starting blocks do you want to explore further?

Replace boxes with balls » Think of the opposite version of what you are doing now. If you are working on boxes, try creating rounder options.

Go on a hike » Often a shift in location or setting can prompt creative solutions. Walk out of your office or plan an off-site retreat. Go somewhere else for a day. Work in a coffee shop.

Recharge your batteries » Take a break when you are stuck on a problem. Set the work aside. A short break or escape can be an effective technique to get your innovative edge back.

Be alone » Listen to your inner reflections. Go for a brainstorming walk. Exercise alone. Don't listen to or watch the news for a day. Cut yourself off from any distractions and become aware of your own deep wisdom. Record your ideas on your way to and from work.

Brew a brainstorm » Ask the most creative people around you for their ideas. Brainstorm with a co-worker.

Rephrase the question » Think of other ways to describe your challenge. Ask yourself what the simplest way out would be. Ask questions without a solution. Ask brainless questions. Then ask some more.

Hear voices » Turn on a radio at random times and listen for "pointers". Remember your imaginings.

Think like a child » Present your challenge to a child. Play with toys in your workplace whenever you become stuck. Have more fun. Be sillier than normal. Laugh more, worry less.

Create a think-tank room » Remodel your work space. Use creative thinking methods. Use metaphors and images when describing your ideas.

Block off time » Arrive at work earlier than the others. Take short daydreaming breaks. Declare a no e-mail zone.

Do random reading » Stroll around a bookstore while thinking about your challenge. Open a magazine and free-connect with a word or image. Decorate your office with touching quotes and images. Read weird books that have nothing to do with your work.

Write, write, write » Trust your gut feeling more. Write down your ideas when you wake up. Take five minutes and write as many ideas as you can think of. Keep an idea notebook.

Repeat your successes » Do more of what already helps you to be creative. Remember your dreams and write them down.

Prototype now » Pilot your idea, even if it is not all set. Test existing limitations. Conduct more experiments and tests. Set a time-line, make a plan, and try something out!

Set a deadline » Give yourself a deadline – and stick to it. Do what is necessary to create a sense of pressure. Have shorter meetings. Decide, "I shall accomplish this in half the time".

Choose to lead » Know that it is possible to make a difference. Eliminate all unnecessary official procedures and admin tasks. Sign up other people in your most captivating plan.

Create an image wall » Put up pictures that move you. Create a compelling vision of what you want to get done. Use this as an "idea piggy bank".

Divide and conquer » Divide your idea into component parts. Then rethink each part. Make drawings of different parts of your ideas. Make connections between apparently disconnected things.

Write note cards » Jot down ideas anytime and everywhere. Ideas are fleeting; therefore, write them down. Capture all your ideas.

Keep notes in meetings » Listen deeply and always search for new ideas. Draw little light bulbs on pages where you wrote down ideas that made a light go on for you.

Challenge everything » Look for three alternatives to every solution you use. Ask, "What is the worst that could happen if I fail?"

B Standing on the wisdom of many generations

"It ain't what you don't know that gets you into trouble. It's what you know for sure that just ain't so."

– MARK TWAIN

The question that will help you focus your awareness this week is: How can I research and present what I know as truths?

Our false creativity can become hopeless and narrow-minded because it longs for certainty. It may cling to the old and familiar, even if this is no longer relevant.

Recognising your allies

If you think back or read about what you have written about your journey thus far, you will discover that you have been developing new allies. They have been actively or silently supporting you on your quest. These people have become your companions on the one hand and sparring partners on the other. They function as your conscience and bring comic relief. You find yourself using them as sounding boards; exchange with them brings hidden ideas to the front.

Think about the people (and animals) journeying with you. See how different ones fulfil different needs during your journey towards your goal.

Become aware of the traveller-ally relationships developing in your life. Many memorable quests have such relationships: Sherlock Holmes and Dr Watson, Don Quixote and his squire, James Bond and Miss Moneypenny, Batman and Robin, Luke Skywalker and a whole range of robots.

Your inner ally is often expressed through dreams. This reminds you of the hidden or suppressed parts of your personality that need healing in order to live your authentic self. Allies show you the strong inner forces that are supporting you on your quest.

Take a moment and list the allies that are in your life. Some will be supporting you; others will be sparring with you. Some are sounding boards; others travel companions. List them all.

Mistakes as sources of insight

Nobody likes making mistakes, but the American author and philosopher Elbert Hubbard said the biggest mistake you can make in life is to always fear that you will make one. Making mistakes is part of life and it is necessary to live, learn and gain experience. Most of us do not like making mistakes because we feel embarrassed, and these feelings prevent us from admitting, learning and carrying on with life.

When making a mistake, accept, relax and enjoy

The other day my sister told me a wonderful story about their tennis coach. She is an older lady who used to be a professional tennis player and who now coaches younger tennis players. Her motto is: Whenever you make a mistake on the court, shout in your head (or out loud if you need to): Accept! Combine it with a ritual such as hitting your racket into your left hand or bumping your head against the racket for your brain to get the sign to accept and get back into the game as soon as possible. Waste no time feeling embarrassed or ashamed because your component will use the moment to get an advantage over you.

Our daughter is a wonderful creative soul who played goal shooter for her u/12 netball team. It is a huge responsibility for a 12-year-old to throw the ball through the ring once the rest of the team succeeded in getting the ball into the goal circle. One day, she was missing one goal after the other while the parents around the court as well as her teammates were becoming frustrated.

The more the tension grew, the more she was affected by it and the less she could get the ball through the ring. During the break Nico went to her, gave her a hug, whispered something into her ear and the game continued. In no time she scored six goals! Everybody cheered. The other parents became very curious about the magic words Nico had said to her. He just smiled at her and gave her the thumbs-up sign.

Only later that night did she tell me what he said, "Relax and enjoy, it's only a game".

When making a mistake, learn from it

A maths teacher explained that his father always scolded and shamed him when he was struggling with maths at school. Later at college he overcame his fear of maths and majored in it. He ended up being a maths teacher. He decided to use his own negative experience to create a new way of teaching maths. Whenever a student made a mistake, he would announce, "Way to go! That an excellent mistake!" He then would help the student to understand the concept. When the student finally understood, he would ask three key questions:

- What was your mistake?
- What made you think this was true?
- What is in fact true?

Once the student could answer these three questions clearly and completely, he did a little role-play to reinforce the concept. Next, he and the student would switch roles. He as teacher would then make the mistake and the student needed to take him through the process.

"Making mistakes simply means you are learning faster."
– WESTON H AGOR

C Open to my inner source of knowledge

"Deep inside of you is a 'Guru' with the wisdom of the entire Universe!"
– ERIN FALL HASKELL

Your last core question of the week is: How can I trust that I will find the right knowledge when I need it?

Our false creativity may stand at a great distance from our core self. We no longer know where the outside world stops and we begin. This can deprive us of the opportunity to serve others.

Design the world around you – don't just copy and paste it. Finding typos is easy. Giving feedback and criticising do not take much. Authentic living comes from a connection with your inner artist and creating a new world. Search your heart and see how the world can be. Be open to receive a picture of a new tomorrow and build it.

While journaling, take a moment to celebrate all the new insights and wisdom you have gained over the past six weeks.

Lifelong learning

Lifelong learning feeds an awareness of knowledge. Does any of the following trigger your curiosity? Choose one and try it.

1. Listen to a motivational recording. Or read an uplifting blog. Listen to inspirational music.
2. Register for a class or workshop on something that interests you. Learn a new skill.
3. Draw, sign up for an art class, or produce some art. Buy art supplies and create a piece of art.
4. Play a musical instrument, or take music lessons. Sing for 15 minutes. Hum or whistle a happy tune.
5. Google holiday craft ideas.
6. Try reading some poetry. Or read positive, motivational or inspirational literature.
7. Visit a zoo and read all the information displayed about the animals.

Read extensively

Reading expands your horizon. It broadens your exposure. It gives you access to knowledge. It fills your mental library with new information. Learning equips you with new knowledge and skills. Maintaining an awareness of news, breakthroughs and trends expands your range of knowledge tools.

Do daydreaming

Free forms of cognitive functions such as *daydreaming* can help you arrive at fresh insights. It allows you to use your imagination and creativity.

Let your mind wander. When you are not focusing on anything specific, it increases your imagination. You may have several ideas in your head that you need to connect, but this will only happen once you relax your mind and allow it to make those connections. In other words, you can become your most creative self when you are daydreaming.

Task: Ask why questions

- If you often think about *the source of your knowledge,* ask yourself: Why can I only get moving when I know why I do something?
- If you almost never think about *the source of your knowledge,* ask yourself: Why don't I look at what's up before I go into action?

Reflection: Checking in on my creativity

- How often did you manage to do your journaling?
- What light bulb moments did you have?
- Where in the week did you experience a special moment?
- What did you struggle with?
- What are you discovering about your authentic creativity?

For the more adventurous

- **Fragments box »** Design a fragments box. With this project you will put fragments of wisdom into a box, helping you to construct a presentation of things (you think) you know.
- **Visualising a quote »** Make a collage about a quote you like. Take someone else's words of wisdom and turn them into something visually inspiring.
- **Wild invention »** Think up a wild invention. This invention should do something that will make you happier — no matter what that is.

SEVEN
Recognising the full worth of my playground

I am supported by how I organise my things.

Structure – my longing for regularity

This week, you will explore structure in your environment. How does the "hive" in which you live help you with the uncertainty of not having a place of your own or not finding a place for yourself? The exercises of this week will help you to explore if you need to tear down your current order. You will also seek to create new order and regularity to support you in your rise to your potential. The promise is a supporting order in which you can rest.

> *"When we want something, all the universe conspires in helping us to achieve it."*
> – PAULO COELHO

I am supported by how I organise my things.

I push and pull towards an optimal environment.

I create order and tidy up.

Life conspires to help me.

What to expect this week: Final preparations before taking a leap

Week 7 is your preparation for a major challenge. It will feel as if the forces trying to block you are closing in, as if the challenges and temptations are overwhelming you.

It will feel as if this road of trials is an ever-rising road without end. It will feel as if the obstacles are pushing you to breaking point. This week may cause you to feel that there is a conspiracy to block your progress. Keep on focusing on building supportive structures around you.

You are exploring who you are authentically and you are determined to live that way. But, you will also experience resistance and struggling. The stakes feel extremely high. The intensity is rising.

Your allies, both in the past and those around you now, will help you with the insights you need.

The symbolic "cave" Little Hans must enter represents many things in his story. It can be an actual location where a frightful danger lies, or it could be an inner conflict that he has not faced until now. As Little Hans approaches the cave he must make final preparations before taking a leap into the great unknown.

At the threshold to the cave, Little Hans may once again face the same doubts and fears that surfaced with his first call to adventure. He may need some time to reflect upon his journey. He may need a break to ponder the treacherous road ahead in order to find the courage to continue. This brief breathing space is necessary because of the hugeness of the trial that awaits him.

My authentic playground

My authentic playground is a space where I can enjoy everything that my surroundings have to offer. Here I can sit back and do what I was born to do.

I like the idea that I do not have to think about arranging my resources myself.

However, I see the possibilities and opportunities in everything around me.

Everything seems to serve me and provide me with the means to achieve success.

I sail through life with an almost unconscious ease, finding that life always conspires to help me. Coincidence does not exist because everything comes to me "naturally".

Examining my "hive"

The "hive" in which you live consists of structures, processes, rituals, conventions, frameworks, patterns, constructions and arrangements. Take a moment to examine the structures of your "hive" by exploring at least five of the following:

- The structures in your immediate environment
- The processes that govern your immediate environment
- The rituals that form part of your immediate environment
- The conventions you adhere to in your immediate environment
- The frameworks that guide your immediate environment

- The patterns underlying your immediate environment
- The constructions that make up your immediate environment
- The arrangements that direct your immediate environment.

Look at the notes you have made and ask:

- Is it natural?
- Does it support who I am?
- Is it organic or forced?

Your false playground is sometimes a frustrating space in which you are forced to work and perform. This can lead to fighting or avoiding (out of principle) in order to side-step a restrictive environment.

Ⓐ Push and pull towards an optimal environment

"The mark of our time is its revulsion against imposed patterns."
– MARSHALL MCLUHAN

Why not tear this "order" apart and see what happens?

In the book *Unstuck: A Tool for Yourself, Your Team, and Your World*, Keith Yamashita and Sandra Spataro suggested that our emotional symptoms are road signs to structural change, and that these symptoms will help us get unstuck. This list of symptoms is the result of an order that does not support us.

Read through the list of feelings and the suggestions they make about how you can "break" the current order.

Overwhelmed

When your life does not have structure and processes in place you can feel overwhelmed. You feel rudderless when you do not know what to do next. Everything seems like too much work. There are too many moving parts and not enough resources. If you do not change this situation you will not be able to tap into your own talent.

What to tear down and what to build: What can you do to minimise "process loss" in your life? What structures and systems can help you to coordinate activities, clarify roles and ensure efficient hand-overs?

Exhausted

You become exhausted when you try to fix parts of a system without bringing them into balance. What you need is to build a prototype of the end state. Without clarity about your goals, you will end up cynical.

What to tear down and what to build: We often get stuck because we cannot see the end state. When this happens, it is unclear what steps we need to take to get there. What prototype can you form of your destination? Make a drawing. Create a scenario. Create a room. Clear out a store room and build that prototype.

Directionless and hopeless

When you lack strategy you will feel directionless. If your aspirations are not clear you will put in an effort but there will be no direction. You will be busy but not effective. You will tick off things on your to-do list without being guided by the "big picture".

You become hopeless when you lack a central purpose. It feels as if you are spinning. You don't have a feeling of reward and no sense of achievement.

What to tear down and what to build: Write down your answers to the following questions to clarify your driving ambition: What must I accomplish before I will feel successful? What is my biggest contribution?

These questions will help you define why you do what you do. Create symbols and stories in your environment to "publish" your vision.

Battle-torn

When the structures around you do not help you interact with people you feel battle-torn. You feel as if you and the people around you just cannot get along. There is almost no energy left to focus on challenges outside the group. This friendly fire can bring the toughest of us to our knees. Your structure should keep your attention on the real task at hand.

What to tear down and what to build: Look at the informal and formal roles you are playing in your interaction with people. How can you "reassign" yourself to new roles? In which process in your environment could you formally renegotiate new roles for yourself?

Worthless

When you do not know how to recognise good work, you start to feel worthless. You feel sabotaged by muddy expectations and moving targets. You need to clarify what the indicators are for amazing work.

What to tear down and what to build: How do you measure and reward your behaviour? Are you rewarding A while hoping for B? What incentives can you put in place that would be aligned with your vision? Build an environment that appreciates, respects, acknowledges and encourages you.

Alone

If your environment does not support a culture of sticking together, your life can feel like "herding cats". Are you structuring your life to create close-knit units? What structures are necessary to create synchronicity and a feeling of working together?

What to tear down and what to build: Culture has to do with "the way we do things around here". What systems can you put in place that make it easier for you to do the right thing? How are your buildings, systems and environment shaping and supporting your routines?

Create leverage through structure

Journal about your environment. Or talk to your friends, family, colleagues and/or team members. Think about the following questions:

- What is holding you back from getting more done?
- What blockers are there in your life? Are there any bottlenecks or barriers you can remove?
- What resources or processes would help you to move as fast as you want to move?

The answers to these questions can help you to create systems that enable speed.

Our disengaged false playground can look at itself from a distance and see itself as someone who is unable and disempowered to change their circumstances. Often, this person over-analyses the pros and cons of the situation.

B Creating order and tidying up

"You never change things by fighting the existing reality. To change something, build a new model that makes the existing model obsolete."
— BUCKMINSTER FULLER

How can we create order and regularity to help ourselves rise to our potential?

Our friend Pieter Kloppers, head of the Centre for Student Communities at Stellenbosch University, tells a story about playing beach volleyball.

When his children were younger he often found himself in a situation where children and adults wanted to play volleyball on the beach.

He explains: "Whenever there was a volleyball game I would always volunteer to be the captain of my team. Before the game I would get my team together and divide the field into blocks. Then I would put our best player in the block I think is the most important. Then I would tell the more inexperienced player, 'Whenever the ball is in your block just hit it as hard a possible into the air'. My final instruction for my best player was, 'If you ever play out of your block, I'll kill you'.

Then Pieter explained what happened next. At the beginning of the game, the other team would play much better. Their best player would be all over the field and overpower his team. His more inexperienced players would drop the ball or not even react when the ball was in their block of the field. But, and this is the important part, as the games goes on, his team's weaker players would become stronger and the other team's star player would become exhausted. And then his team would win the game.

Take time and examine the "block" you are playing in. How can you create structure around your time, your use of time, your working space and your role to support who you are?

Structures support your authentic self in its development and functioning.

Ask yourself:

- What changes can I make to my physical space and resources to support me?
- What changes can I make to the use and structuring of my time to support me?
- What changes can I make to the way I vitalise and spend my energy to support me?
- What changes can I make to my functional role to support me in terms of my goals?

Structure for your needs

Take time to attend to your personal needs. Dare to think of yourself for a change. Think of what you really need, even if it feels or sounds childish.

Focusing on self-care » What have you done in the past that boosted your well-being? Maybe it was a massage, coffee at your favourite coffee shop or listening to feel-good music.

Creating a safe environment » What type of setting helps you to relax and to be playful and creative? For some it is a group activity like a gym class. For others it might be a one-on-one art class.

Clearing blockages » What have you done in the past to move beyond emotional obstacles? Who helped you with that? For some it's writing in a journal. For others it's meditating or going for counselling.

Our disengaged false playground can cast everything in stone. Even when things change, the conceived structures are maintained. Even if everything else changes, you may keep on believing that what supported you in the past will keep on supporting you in the future.

To sustain your authentic story you need supportive systems and structures. You must break down blockages and create new structures. Your environment should be designed to help you. It should be organised in a way that allows the energy in your life to flow.

Think of your habitat as an airport building. Everything is designed to let people proceed through it. Think of irrigation channels. They are built to let the water flow through gravity.

What supportive structures can you build? What dysfunctional structures can you break down? The exercise below will help you think about these questions.

Creating a supportive environment

The function of the structures you build is to support your rise in potential. It is a worthwhile activity to revisit these structures, challenge some and create new ones. Use the following ideas to kindle your imagination:

1. **Declutter your cupboards:** Mess causes stress. Go through your wardrobe and let go of what you no longer need.
2. **Get enough sleep:** Go to bed early. Sometimes a good night's sleep can be the best investment in the following day.
3. **Give your mornings a makeover:** Get up earlier so you can have some quiet time to yourself before the day begins.
4. **Make one positive change in your diet:** Change one thing to improve your diet.
5. **Change your appearance:** Get a haircut, perhaps a totally different style. This can be refreshing and help change your outlook.
6. **Clean something:** Clean something you use every day.
7. **Get moving:** Make time to exercise or go to the gym. Take the stairs instead of the lift, or do some jumping jacks in your office.
8. **Try out something new:** Experiment with new foods or recipes.
9. **Buy a plant to pretty up your place:** Buy a new plant for your garden, house or office.
10. **Simplify your life:** Make something easier in your life. Let go of something.

C Life conspires to help me

"When patterns are broken, new worlds emerge."
– TULI KUPFERBERG

How can we sit back and enjoy the support that our surroundings offer us?

Core questions to create your authentic playground

Regularity » What regularity or consistency can I create to support me? How can I create order to help me rise to my potential? What changes can I make to manage my time better?

Resources » How can I arrange the resources around me so that I can rest in them?

Conventions » What conventions in my environment should I change to serve me and provide me with the means to achieve success?

Flow » What can I do to minimise "process loss" in my life? What new order is needed to create sync and a feeling of working together with the people around me? What new processes can help to manage my immediate environment and to let the energy flow in my life?

Empowerment » What frameworks in my immediate environment will help me balance all the different parts?

Prototype » What prototype or scenario of my destination can I form? What symbols and stories can I create in my environment to "publish" my vision?

Interaction » What arrangements in my environment will help me to interact better with people? How can I construct my life to create a supporting unit around me? What structures and systems can help me coordinate activities and ensure efficient hand-overs?

Roles » What processes in my environment will help me renegotiate new roles for myself?

Incentives » What incentives can I put in place that would be be aligned with my objectives? How can I build an environment that appreciates, acknowledges and encourages me? What systems can I put in place to make it easier for me to do the right thing?

Physical space » How are the buildings and systems in my environment shaping and supporting my routines? What changes can I make to my physical space and resources to support me?

Creative space » Which rituals in my environment could help me relax and be more playful and creative?

Productivity » Which patterns in my environment allow me to move optimally? How is the structure of my meetings energising or blocking my productivity? Are there structures that are creating frustrating work spaces, hampering my performance? How can I redesign these structures?

Structure exercise

Identify » Think of six of your most visible gifts. Add short descriptions.

Support » Think of incidents where your gifts supported you in such a way that they made you a better or more efficient person.

Unpack » Unpack the support. Who? What? How? Where? How did structures help you perform or function in the best possible manner with the least waste of time and effort?

Task: Ask why questions

- If you often think about *the structure of your environment*, ask yourself: Why do I think everything has to have its place?
- If you almost never think about *the structure of your environment*, ask yourself: Why do I not care about the right order of things?

Reflection: Checking in on my playground

- How often did you manage to do your journaling?
- Where can you create structures to support your authentic self?
- Where in the week did you experience resistance in your quest to an authentic self?
- What did you struggle with?
- Where could you see integration between this journey and your life journey? Did you experience any synchronicity (meaningful coincidences, or things, seemingly unrelated, happening on the same timeline)?

For the more adventurous

- **Recreate the picture** » Collage a painting. Start by creating a simple, abstract painting on paper, or choose a beautiful postcard or picture. Then tear this painting up and create another. Think about how you felt when you had to tear up the first painting and which one you liked more.

- **Clutter collage** » Create a clutter collage. Are things cluttering up your life? In this project, use words and pictures to show the clutter hampering your progress.

- **Create a calming collage** » Choose images that you find soothing, calming or even meditative. Combine them to create an attractive collage that can help you to relax.

- **Tree description** » Draw or describe yourself as a tree. Let the roots be represented by those things that give you strength, and let the leaves be represented by those things that you are trying to change.

EIGHT
Recognising the full worth of my biography

I am proud of what I have been able to experience.

Insight – my inner recognition

This week, we will help you unlock your inner world. You will be asked to listen and reflect in order to know yourself. You will be asked to face the fear of not understanding yourself or the fear of not feeling normal. You will discover the quests you can go on or revisit those you have been on to find out who you really are. This week, you will gratefully accept what life has given you and be happy with who you are becoming.

> *"When we deny our stories, they define us. When we own our stories, we get to write a brave new ending."*
> – BRENÉ BROWN

I am proud of what I have been able to experience.

I am seeking self-knowledge and self-realisation.

I am investigating to solve "the mystery of me".

I accept all the puzzle pieces of my story.

What to expect this week: Face to face with my deepest fears

Week 8 is the most difficult week of the entire process. This is where you choose to face the "dragon" in your life. You need to do this on your own. You have a feeling that this is a matter of life and death.

To complicate matters, you will hit rock bottom this week. You will fail miserably in your first attempts to embrace your authentic self. You will come face to face with your deepest fears. The demons will be very real and powerful.

This will lead to a much-needed self-revelation. An epiphany. Be on the lookout for that.

This is the week to let go of the false self – to let your ego die.

Enter the dark night of the soul.

Enter the crisis, the seemingly bottomless pit.

Do the final push and make new plans to reach your goal.

Little Hans's ultimate test may be a dangerous physical test or a deep inner crisis that he must face in order to survive. Whether it is facing his greatest fear or most deadly foe, he must draw upon all of his skills and his experiences gathered on this path to the innermost cave in order to overcome his most difficult challenge.

Only through some form of "death" can Little Hans be reborn. Through "dying" he will experience a symbolic restoration to life that somehow grants him greater power or insight. This is necessary for him to fulfil his destiny or reach his journey's end. This is the high point of Little Hans's journey where everything he holds dear is put on the line. If he fails, he will either die or life as he knows it will never be the same again.

This week you are called upon to face the shadow. The shadow represents the energy of the dark side. It is your rejected, repressed or unexpressed thoughts, feelings and beliefs. You will confront deep and dark parts of yourself. These parts feed on trauma or guilt. Maybe these parts have been suppressed and driven deep into your inner self. From there, emotions can grow into monstrous and destructive things.

Your shadow represents your thoughts and emotions that are so damaged that contact is lost with external reality. That will hamper and harm you.

On your journey, the function of the shadow is to try and oppose you. It provides you with a worthy challenge in your fight to reach your authentic self.

Sometimes the shadow reveals itself in you. It represents the obstacles you face in reaching your goal, but it can also represent your hidden and repressed feelings, thoughts and beliefs.

You need to reflect on the highs and lows of the past to gain new insight and accept what life has brought you.

We are introducing a life-line exercise later to assist you with this. It will help you to understand what it is you need to break with or leave behind. Your new identity could evolve from the alternative story; it can jumpstart a whole new beginning. This is the start of writing a brave new ending to your story.

Authentic object

This week we ask of you to be on the lookout for an ornament, amulet or magical object. In many myths and movies the hero receives a symbolic "power object" that gives them magical powers and makes them invulnerable. Obviously, the power of the object does not lie on the surface.

Think of what is sacred to you. Is there something that represents who you truly are? Have you received or rediscovered something in your life? Is there something you can carry with you that will remind you of what you are learning, or what you need to learn? Are there old objects you should get rid of?

My authentic biography

Read the following description of your authentic biography. Become aware of how much of this is true of you at this moment. How much of it is a deep longing you have? What emotions are awakened by this description?

My authentic biography gratefully accepts what life has given me. This includes not only the pluses and minuses, but also the lessons.

It makes me happy to know why I am who I am. The "lesser" traits in me no longer bother me.

My authentic biography has a picture of the history that has turned me into the remarkable being I have become. I look around me and see that everything is good! Apparently, I have received the right ingredients at the right time in my life. This has enabled me to learn everything about being happy and full of love. This is why I can love myself as well as love others.

Write down in your journal what happened to you while reading this description of your authentic biography.

Brave new ending

Read the following instructions and do the exercise before proceeding:

Close your eyes and replay your whole life as a movie in your head. Begin as far back as you can remember. Let each chapter come to you. View the scenes from the outside – almost like a moviegoer. See how the light as well as the dark scenes moulded you. See how each one was important to shape you into who you are today. Receive each moment of your life's movie. Don't look away. Resist any criticism of the main character (you). If you feel shame, acknowledge it and then send it away. Each chapter was necessary for your growth. Each chapter made you uniquely who you are.

After you have watched as many scenes in your head as you feel comfortable with, thank life (Life) for everything it has given you. Receive all that has happened to you as a gift.

A   Seeking self-knowledge and self-realisation

"These are the only genuine ideas; the ideas of the shipwrecked. All the rest is rhetoric, posturing, farce. He who does not really feel himself lost, is without remission; that is to say, he never finds himself, never comes up against reality."

– JOSÉ ORTEGA Y GASSET

This week, you will be busy with a question: On what quests do I have to go in order to find out who I am?

Our false biography comes up against itself. The way we think about how our inner world was formed sometimes fights and clashes with itself. Then we are unable to understand the logic of our own background.

It is also true of other people

A while ago we were at a party. I am a very good listener. One man at this party told me his whole life story. How he grew up poor, on the wrong side of the railroad tracks, with an absent mother. He also told me how he always had to fight for himself. How he never received enough attention.

I listened to him with empathy and deeply validated what he said. Somewhere near the end of his story he said he just wanted people to understand that he does not act the way he does because he wants to but that his behaviour stems from his story. The conversation was interrupted when we were called to the dinner table. As an afterthought, I said, "Now that you understand your own story and the effect it is having on your behaviour, the trick in life is to understand that everyone has a story."

The man looked at me, frowned and said, "No, no! Now you're asking too much of me."

Understanding that you do not always act the way you want to, is a start. Being worried about how your past is influencing your relationships is one thing; to understand that the same is true of other people is something completely different. It is at this point that we start to broaden our understanding of the world. The challenge is to stand still and become aware of the fact that you are looking at the world through a broken lens.

You deserve that other people will confirm you; that people close to you will handle you with care; that they won't hurt you again where life has already hurt you.

But you should also know that this is true for everyone else.

It has everything to do with how the brain works.

Psychologist Carl Jung, a contemporary of Freud, said, "When an inner situation is not made conscious it appears on the outside as fate". If something is happening in you and you are not aware of it, it becomes a reality outside of you. It becomes a fate that controls your life. Just entertain the thought that this inside consciousness could be the trouble. The pain you are experiencing in life is your own glasses' cracked lenses.

In 1965, the American neuroscientist Dr Paul MacLean proposed a theory that the brain consists of three major "parts". According to him, the brain's functioning can be understood by thinking of these three parts as the reptile brain, the mammalian brain and the frontal lobe.

Humans have a spinal cord with a reptile brain at the top. The stem from the brain to the spinal cord is the reptile brain. That is what lizards have. From this reptile brain the four Fs stem – function, feeding, flight and fright, as well as reproduction.

Above and around the reptile brain is the mammalian brain. That is the brain that mammals – such as dogs, cows and elephants – have. But you also have a frontal lobe. This is the part of your brain that can think that you think.

Why is this important? Our wounds, our hurts, and the things that make our relationships complicated can hide in any of these three levels in our brain.

The small brain fights or flees

The function of the reptile brain is to keep the organism alive. There are certain things that Mother Nature wisely felt she could not leave for us to do ourselves, such as breathing and our heartbeat. These functions happen without us consciously thinking about them.

The reptile brain also instructs the organism to help us when our lives are in danger or when we feel threatened. As soon as the reptile brain feels unsafe, you either fight or flee.

Have you talked to a friend and the next moment he or she simply "switches off"? He turns away or she walks out? That is when it suddenly becomes unsafe to be together.

We have needs in our relationships, but often, through what we do and say, we make it unsafe for the reptile brain to be in the relationship.

Remake your life: a lifeline exercise

It is always helpful to reflect on your life's journey. When doing this, many people discover that they are already living parts of their dream. People are always surprised when they discover there have been times (or at least moments or events) when they have felt fully alive and showed their authentic side to the world.

Do the following exercise and be on the lookout for you own alternative story. Somewhere in your story you will find your unexplored longings, your authentic self.

Below is a simple lifeline exercise that will help you discover your own aliveness, and how to continue living your dreams.

What does your lifeline say about you?

1. Draw a simple graph

Draw a scale from 0-10 on the vertical axis (0 indicating feeling dull and depressed; 10 feeling vibrant and alive). Put your age from birth to now on the horizontal axis.

Start filling in your lifeline by rating your aliveness at this moment.

Go to your age (horizontal axis) and rate your aliveness (vertical axis) by asking: How alive did I feel at each moment? Take into account your work, family and social life.

On the scale from 0-10, mark those moments in your life when you felt most alive. Try to remember the circumstances – for example, quitting your job to start your own business, being in a fulfilling relationship, working flexible hours, or feeling like you had a purpose in life.

2. Remember and mark the moments when you felt really depressed and dull

Mark those times that were lows in your life. Try to remember the circumstances – for example, having small kids, being in a job that did not energise you, or being in an abusive relationship at work and/or at home.

3. Give your aliveness theme a name

Use a touch of humour and creativity when choosing a name. You can even name it after a Disney character or animal, characters from books, stories or movies, or even from your faith tradition. I have heard names such as Brave Heart, Superman/Superwoman, Happy Feet, Owl and Sunflower. The trick is to pick up on that golden thread, take on the challenge to become fully alive again and design your life around this.

Give this alternative story a name and internalise the theme you have recognised. I believe that your alternative story and the themes you have rated as extremely happy or ecstatic are part of your authentic self showing itself.

This represents the lifeline we could have had if we were brought up in a perfectly supportive environment. It is who we could have become in an ideal world.

In our alternative story, we often act counterintuitively. In these moments of aliveness we follow our original path. Through these "sparkling events" parts of our authentic self can shine through. It is for us to identify them, to see them for what they are and not to dismiss them. We need to see this pattern in our journey and strengthen it. Often, it starts with a very thin or dotted line. Sometimes we need outside witnesses to help us see it and to help us realign our lives with the dots leading us to our authentic self. We need supportive systems to protect this path, like a fence around a young tree, allowing it to grow without disturbances or danger.

4. Name your 'shadow'

"We stopped looking for monsters under our bed when we realised that they were inside us."
– CHARLES DARWIN

For many people it is difficult to confront their shadow – that side of them that they want to hide from themselves (and the rest of the world). But, go into your shadow side (Jung will be very proud of you!) and name your shadow story. Look your monster in the eye and call it, him or her by their real name: rejection, anger, loneliness, depression, not being good enough. To tame it, give it a nickname such as Rescuer, Jekyll and Hyde, Mrs Fixit, Black Dog or Grumpy.

It helps to give this shadow a name. It enables you to examine it from a distance and to get to know it from the outside inwards. So give it a name and, if you want to, also a gender. Is it a thing or a living creature? Draw the creature. What are the characteristics of this creature? What is its strategy? Where or when did it/he/she enter your life? When or where did it leave?

Understand that this shadow is not living inside you; it is only visiting you as an external entity, separate from you as a human being. This means you can fight this shadow, even conquer it. The shadow joined you somewhere on your journey because you have done some things to make this shadow feel at home. The shadow also taught you quite a few skills. Fighting the shadow, you have acquired some muscle (skills, attitudes and commitment) that is very unique to your journey.

5. Stop and think

When or where did you conquer your shadow? What was the setting? Who else was involved? Who or what supported you on this journey? What skills, attitudes and commitments flowed from this challenge?

Maybe you want to give this aliveness theme a name as well.

6. Reflect and write down all the light bulb moments

Study the correlations and circumstances around both themes – dullness and aliveness – by asking the following questions:

- When were you embracing your aliveness?
- Where did you live at the time?
- Where did you work at the time?
- What did you do on a typical day?
- With whom did you spend time?
- What did you believe in?
- What do your aliveness times have in common, and what do your bad times (monsters) have in common? Identify the powers between the lines or themes.

Use these insights to design your life around them and to become fully alive.

B Investigating to solve "the mystery of me"

"When we are no longer able to change a situation, we are challenged to change ourselves."
– VICTOR FRANKL

This week, you will also be thinking about the following: How can I listen and reflect in order to know who I am?

Our false biography can hamper our development because we think we know who we are. We can form fixed ideas about ourselves. We base this on what we have read or heard about ourselves. This apparent "self-knowledge" can become a fake authority on our life's journey.

Your brain is much more than a human reptile brain. You also have a mammalian brain. This is the part of the brain from where our need to be part of the "herd" originates. The mammalian brain produces many of our feelings. A dog can be happy or sad, and a cow can be excited or scared. The mammalian brain is the place where we experience our feelings.

The trouble with the mammalian brain is that it cannot distinguish between yesterday and today. A dog that was beaten when it was a puppy is a dog that was beaten. The mammalian brain cannot understand time. All the pain we have already experienced lies in the present in the mammalian brain. It does not become any less there. Time actually does not heal all wounds. No, as time goes by, the hurt in the mammalian brain becomes more, not less.

How do you know if you have been hurt? People overreact. You overreact.

My husband Nico tells the following story:

> When our daughter was about two years old, she no longer wanted to sleep in her baby bed; she insisted on a real bed. Great! Until we discovered she could get out of that bed without any difficulty.
>
> One evening we invited people over for dinner. We ate the starter with our daughter also sitting at the table. Between the starter and the main course, Elsa took her and put her to bed.
>
> I, the introvert, tried to make small talk at the table while Elsa, the extrovert, was tucking in the child. I don't know why we did it this way, but that's what had happened.
>
> When Elsa returned, we dished up the main course. The conversation around the table was flowing again.
>
> From my place at the table, I could see our daughter's bedroom door down the passage. The next moment she peeked around the corner.
>
> And from this point onwards, Elsa and I tell different stories about the evening.
>
> My version sounds like this ...
>
> Annoyed and in front of everyone, Elsa said to me: "You can also do something for a change."
>
> Reluctantly, I stood up and went to our daughter. I picked her up, put her back in bed and sat down next to her. I continued sitting there until she was asleep. Still, I did not get up. Breathing deeply, I tried to calm myself. Big fright. I couldn't believe Elsa just did that to me!
>
> Eventually, I joined the guests again.
>
> When the people had left, we tried to unravel what had happened.
>
> All wounds are in the present. My wounds are in the present.

Elsa stepped on my wounds when she reprimanded me in front of other people. That is my wound: to be criticised in front of others.

Here is Elsa's side of the story …

She is the middle child of six children. Growing up, she, like everyone else in the family, had to accommodate all the other people in the house. As a child, she experienced that her contribution was not always noticed or appreciated.

So, when our daughter peeked around the corner and I did not respond immediately, Elsa thought: I made the food, put our child to bed and dished up. I cannot understand why Nico did not notice and appreciate that.

We were two people with two totally different wounds. These are two totally different stories. But both our mammalian brains were activated at the same time, causing us to go to our wounds.

Now record your particular story

How would you tell the story of your life to yourself? What would your autobiography sound like? One key part of who you are is your life story. Mapping out your story may help you make some changes for the future.

Choose your own story plot

Read through the following list of basic story plots compiled by Ronald B Tobias (*20 Master Plots: And How to Build Them*, 2012). Which one resonates with your authentic self? How would you describe your new life plot?

- **The quest:** I am searching for a person, place or thing, tangible or intangible (that is, immortality).
- **The adventure:** I am going in search of my fortune, and since fortune is never found at home, I search for it somewhere over the rainbow.
- **The pursuit:** I am literally playing hide-and-seek, I am chasing someone.
- **The rescue:** I am looking for someone or something.
- **The escape:** I am confined against my will, wanting to escape.
- **The riddle:** I am looking for clues to find the hidden meaning of something in question that is mysterious, confusing or ambiguous.
- **The rivalry:** I am competing for some object or goal against another person (my rival).
- **The underdog:** I am competing for an object or goal but I have a great disadvantage and I am faced with overwhelming odds.
- **The metamorphosis:** My outside is actually changing from one form into another (reflecting my inner mental, emotional and intellectual identity).
- **The transformation:** There is a change in me as I journey through a stage of life that moves me from one significant way of living to another.
- **The maturation:** I am facing a problem that is part of growing up, and dealing with it. I am emerging into a state of adulthood (going from innocence to experience).
- **The love:** I am overcoming the obstacles to love that keep me from engaging in true love.

- **The sacrifice:** I am taking action that is motivated by a higher purpose such as love, honour, charity or humanity.
- **The discovery:** I am overcoming an upheaval in my life, and thereby discovering something important buried within me. I am thus getting a better understanding of life.

C I accept all the puzzle pieces of my story

"The awareness of the ambiguity of one's highest achievements (as well as one's deepest failures) is a definite symptom of maturity."
– PAUL TILLICH

How can we gratefully accept what life has given us and be happy with who we have become?

Our disengaged false biography can start looking at us from a distance. We may then regard the stories of our lives as something inevitable. We might feel it is easier to accept who we are if we don't think about the forming of our inner world.

Nico shares the following:

It was in a small lecture room in Stellenbosch with 10 other participants that a challenge came to me. Like many people from my generation, I have been trying to figure out who I am for many years. I was attending a course on awareness presented by Marc Grond. At age 45, I felt that I had pretty much figured out who I was and why I am the way I am. But, I did not like some of the things I "knew" about myself. Some of my "traits" did not sit comfortably with me. I was ashamed of "the way I was".

What I did not see at that stage was that these solid ideas that I had about myself were constructs that I had built over time and that were now set in stone.

With everyone looking at me, Marc asked me, "Could you imagine that your ideas about yourself, even though you are very sure about them, are false? And that we love you just the way you are?"

To find your authentic self the mask must be taken off. My ideas about myself both disguised and revealed me.

But without this mask I feel naked. It feel as if I am showing too much, if I am too vulnerable. Without my mask I am afraid that I will show too much of my shadow. I am afraid to show things about myself that I don't want to admit.

I need my mask, otherwise I feel too infantile, unguarded, even aggressive. I think I need my mask to protect me from danger. Without my mask I feel at risk, unsafe, almost endangered.

My impenetrable mask is an attempt to make me immune to hurt, shame and attacks. With the appropriate mask I would not be at risk. I will be protected, guarded and fortified. I will not be defenceless against attacks from the outside.

Remember the sparkling events

Make a list of the times when you thought you were your best self. Take a moment and remember what happened, what you did and what the circumstances were.

For example: As a student, you had to organise an event as part of the university's student body. A record number of students attended and the event was a financial success. Now reflect on your contribution: "I networked among the students on campus and sourced sponsors for the event. I delegated the ticket sales to the rest of the committee and supported them in their efforts, but I did not do the sales. I was creative in putting together a very interesting out-of-the-box event."

Look back at positive feedback

Recall the compliments and appreciation you have received. If possible, reread those messages.

Here are examples of messages that we should keep to remind ourselves of our strengths:

- **Message:** "Thank you for chairing the meeting in a way that made people calm down and relax."
- **Message:** "Thank you for being there for me during this very traumatic time in my life. Thank you for all the messages, listening, coffee and even food. You are a wonderful friend!"

Remember the people who have empowered you

Think of the people who believed in you and who showed that they had your best interest in mind. Recall what they said about you and the value you added.

Here is an example: "I remember my first manager wrote a report on my performance. The report said that I was very conscientious and creative, had very good insight in what I was doing and had excellent interpersonal relationships with my customers and colleagues."

Unpack previous successes

List the accomplishments you are most proud of and unpack your own recipe or framework for the success you have achieved.

An example: You studied part-time and completed your degree in a record time. Or you stopped smoking or improved your lifestyle. How did you do this? What motivated you?

Authentic living is intense.

It takes courage to be present. It takes courage to stay in the moment and step up. It takes courage to stay awake. It takes courage to cuddle the now and create the future.

To find your authentic self you need to enter the unknown. You need to let go of the world where you feel safe. Aliveness is in the "night world".

We are all multi-storied beings. We are living many parallel stories. On this journey we often only want the light and fight the darkness. We invite enlightenment and fear the night. But uncertainty and crisis will help you to discover that you are both.

Task: Ask why questions

- If you often try *to connect the dots of your life journey,* ask yourself: Why do I give so much attention to my life story?
- If you almost never try *to connect the dots of your life journey,* ask yourself: Why am I not an introspective person?

Memory notebook

Buy yourself a special memory notebook. Choose one of the following exercises and start reflecting on your life, your accomplishments and your victories.

- **Your achievements:** Make a list of your special achievements, no matter how small they may seem. Start an Applause File with thank you notes and comments you received. Start by making a list of 25 accomplishments from the past year.
- **Photographs:** Put some of your favourite photographs in frames and display them.
- **Special memories:** Reflect on: "My most enjoyable memories".
- **Practising gratitude:** Keep a gratitude journal. Reflect on: "I appreciate ..." or "I am grateful for ..."
- **Positive qualities:** Reflect on your positive qualities: "I am ..."
- **Your accomplishments:** Write in a special diary about your accomplishments. Smile and say, "I love myself". Write an appreciative letter to yourself and mail it to yourself.
- **Your successes:** Reflect on your successes: "I can ..."
- **Burning bowl ceremony:** Hold your own burning bowl ceremony to symbolise the removal of negative things from your life. Make a list of all the things that you dislike about your current life situation and that you want to let go of. Write them on small slips of paper. When you have finished writing, burn them all. Now write down the things you want to replace your dislikes with and keep this list with you.

List the things you've done

A done list is the opposite of a to-do list. Make a list of things you have already accomplished. This list of the things you have achieved can act as a reminder of how far you have come. It will remind you of the road you have travelled up to here.

Write a regret letter

Write a letter to your younger self. This is a surprisingly relieving exercise. Make it more than simply a list of things you wish you had known. Tell your younger self about the regrets you have in your life. Apologise for any mistakes that you have made. Confess those opportunities that you let slip through your fingers.

But more than this, reflect on how these difficult times have formed you. What has pain taught you? How did these struggles make you stronger?

This exercise will help you gain a feeling of empowerment by accepting your vulnerable younger self.

Reflection: Checking in on my biography

- How often did you manage to do your journaling?
- Where could you connect the dots while reflecting on your life journey?
- When and where did you experience a special moment during this week that will help you start a new chapter in your story?
- With what did you struggle?
- Where could you clearly see integration between this journey and your life journey? Did you experience any synchronicity (the feeling that there is a reason why events that have no obvious connection are occurring at the same time)?

For the more adventurous

- **Transformation portraits** » Create a transformational portrait series. Transform your perceptions about yourself with this list of self-portrait ideas.
- **Time self-portraits** » Create a past, present and future self-portrait. This drawing or painting should reflect where you have been, who you are today, and how see yourself in the future.
- **Visual autobiography** » Design a visual autobiography. This creative journaling project asks you to look back on your life and make a visual representation of it.
- **Moments timeline** » Create a timeline, and journal on the most significant moments in your life. This timeline will be the story of your life, with the most important moments highlighted visually.
- **Childhood memories** » Paint an important childhood memory. What was a pivotal memory in your childhood? This activity asks you to document it and try to understand why it was so important to you.
- **Heart collage** » Collage your childhood memories in a heart formation.

STAGE 3

Wave
your crown

The last four weeks will focus on your reaction to change and on fitting in.

This awareness will help you to think about movements in you and in others. It will also guide you to become aware of what you show in terms of what is being asked of you.

"When in doubt, choose change."
– LILY LEUNG

NINE
Recognising the full worth of my future

I am prepared for what is coming.

Agility – my capacity to react

This week, you are going to explore your capacity to react. You will become aware of what you as a "wind rooster" do with change. Are you more anxious to be prepared, or to know what the next step is? You will taste a "let's just find out" attitude towards change. You will discover that you can use your reading of the now to form your vision of the future. All of this will guide you to calmly receive the future that is unfolding.

> *"It is neither the strongest of the species that survives, nor the most intelligent. It is the one that is the most adaptable to change."*
>
> – CHARLES DARWIN

I am prepared for what is coming.

I find life at the edge of my comfort zone.

I am mapping future possibilities.

I am calm regardless of what is coming my way.

What to expect this week: Deep transformation

"You must let life flow naturally, for life's secret is patience; you must stop pushing for change and allow things to unfold."
– LEON BROWN

Having survived the life test, you accept the impact this has on your new life. You are claiming back the ownership of your authentic self after facing "death". This week is the time of the final climactic battle – the week of your deep transformation.

Be nimble when "grabbing the sword away before your foes". What you have learned during the past eight weeks is essential to seize the prize you are seeking.

There may be celebration, but there is also the danger of losing the treasure again. Beware of post-battle fatigue.

After defeating the enemy, surviving death and finally overcoming his greatest personal challenge, Little Hans is ultimately transformed into a new state. He emerges from the battle as a stronger person, and often with a prize.

The reward may come in many forms. It might be an object of great importance. It could be a power or a secret. He could receive greater knowledge or insight. It could even be reconciliation with a loved one or an ally. Whatever the treasure, Little Hans must quickly put celebrations aside and prepare for the last leg of his journey.

Also be aware of people, things and systems that by their very nature are changing and recasting themselves the whole time. Shapeshifters take on many forms to toy with your goals and emotions.

This shapeshifting can also play out in your inner world. You need your pragmatism and mental focus as well as your sensitivity, intuition and empathy to survive and to maintain a healthy inner balance.

On your journey, the shapeshifter brings doubt into your story. You will become aware of questions about faithfulness, love and betrayal. At a more innocent level, all of this form part of the normal game of love. In the game of love people display, exaggerate or hide aspects of themselves from one another. We often dress up for the roles we play.

This week it will feel as if the whole world is "shapeshifting" the whole time. As if everything and everyone around you are changing. As if they are playing a game with you. Sometimes charming you, sometimes rejecting you.

This is the game of life. Respond with agility.

My authentic future

Read the following description of your authentic future. Become aware of how much of it is true of you at this moment. How much of it is a deep longing you have? What emotions are awakened by this description?

My authentic future does not need to wait for anything or anticipate anything. My strong presence allows me to be normal, regardless of what is coming my way.

I trust that I am everything I should be. I do what I can and may do.

Come what may, my authentic future sees myself getting out of every situation with great calmness and confidence. I effortlessly sense and move along, without being too concerned or finding this extraordinary. I seem to know what is coming my way. This allows me to be well prepared.

Write in your journal what happened to you while reading this description of your authentic future.

A Finding life at the edge of my comfort zone

"I cannot say whether things will get better if we change; what I can say is they must change if they are to get better."
– GEORG C. LICHTENBERG

Let the following question guide you this week: How do I get to "Let's just find out"?

Your false future has no time to catch its breath because you feel your feet are burning. You are always too busy to be in the present. You feel an overwhelming pressure to save yourself in the midst of anxiety and hostility.

"If you chase two rabbits, you will not catch either one."
– RUSSIAN PROVERB

In *The Different Drum: Community Making and Peace* (1998), M Scott Peck tells a story of a rabbi who got lost in the woods. For months he searched and scouted but could not find his way out. Finally, one day during his hunt for an exit, he encountered a group from his synagogue who had also become lost in the forest. Overjoyed, they exclaimed, "Rabbi, how wonderful we have found you. Now you can lead us out of the woods!"

"I am sorry, I cannot do that," the rabbi replied. "For I am just as lost as you are. What I can do, because I have had more experience of being lost, is to tell you about a thousand ways you cannot get out of these woods."

Change: An emergent approach

Imagine a funky boardroom filled with the senior management of a Cape Town-based international tech company. I was there as the facilitator of a workshop to start a new intervention on change management. The outcome of these three hours with the management would determine the approval of the rest of the project with the other 85 people of the software product development unit.

Nervously excited on the inside but with a calm smile on the outside, I approached them. And to my surprise they almost immediately latched onto the new concepts and started playing along. The energy in the room escalated with lots of interaction, fun and laughter. My heart sang. This was going to be a great project!

In the middle we had a break for coffee.

Before I could find my way out, one of the guys asked me to step into a different board room. He closed the door behind us. Without any small talk or introduction he dropped the bomb. He had a video conference earlier that morning with the company's head office abroad. They told him they have decided to close the Cape Town office. They would be relocating to India. This would take a few months, but in the meantime the office still needed to deliver on their promises. No one else in the office may know of this plan. He needed to carry on as if nothing had happened. They needed to deliver as promised. He needed to carry this secret without disclosing it to his close colleagues and friends. He just thought that I also needed to know this …

Multi-change

Let me start at the very beginning.

A few months earlier I received a phone call from the sponsor of the project. We have worked together on a few projects at different companies. She asked me to assist her with a transition in an IT environment. A meeting was scheduled for the next week, where she would explain the current situation.

After we had greeted each other, she almost immediately grabbed a pen and started to draw her usual diagram and scribble to explain what was going on.

An innovative South African start-up was bought by a multi-national for its IP. At first, this big giant left these "creatives" to carry on in their weird and wonderful ways, creating and developing. After about two or three years, the powers that be decided they did not have enough control and structure, and insisted on changing the unit's name to reflect its relationship with the larger organisation.

Next, they said that if you use our name, you need to adhere to our rules. They rented a smart new office and relocated the unit. Things started changing. First they said: "If you put our name on your door, you need to adhere to our security rules." So they hired a security company, which meant you had to sign in three times and get a tag before you could enter the premises.

Under our name, you also need to adhere to the international standards of recruitment, budgeting and the way you develop products. And by the way, we don't think the products (that we bought the IP of) are relevant any more. We are going to change direction here as well.

The company then saw that these creatives were not that easy to get marching in a straight line. They decided that they needed more direct supervision. They began to manage them hands-on from the other side of the ocean through video conferences at odd hours of the day. With that came different report structures which resulted in new and changed teams. Gone were the teams that have been working together for years and have formed "families".

As the project sponsor explained all of this to me, my head started spinning. I was not sure that I got it all but while I was still struggling to grab it, I heard the following statement, "So it is easy. I want you to spread your magic and enhance their emotional intelligence to fit their high IQ, so that they can deal with the multiple changes."

Multiple changes! These were the multiple change levels that spun around in my head:

- Change from an independent, informal and innovative start-up to highly formal, structured and regulated multinational
- Relocate from an informal setting and venue to a formal, modern, high-security building
- Change from working with familiar teams and informal management to working with restructured teams adapting to new development methodologies
- Cope with management change from local familiar to international unfamiliar, with a different culture and time zone with video conferences
- Drop the expertise and IP, and focus on developing different products
- And in the process, drop your dreams ...

What would the ethical choice be? To go back and continue as if they were going to work for this giant for ever and a day?

So I did what I usually do when this happens. I phoned a friend!

He calmly reminded me, "Remember, it's a cat, not a toaster." I remembered that he had explained it to me before. When something is wrong with a toaster, you can take it apart, see what is going on and fix it, or throw it away and buy a new one. A cat is a bit different. If your cat is "broken", taking it apart won't help you.

Cynefin theory

Working with organisations (with real people in these organisations) Dave Snowdon, with his Cynefin theory, says when you add people to any system, it becomes chaotic and complex ... like cats. Take them through change and they all start doing their own thing, their own survival thing.

One of the things I understand from Snowdon is that you need to be brave enough to dare to prototype. You need to try something that has not been tried before in order to test the water and see whether the cat would like it or not. Whether it would organically survive the complexity.

Brené Brown refers to this as "daring greatly", to be vulnerable and to go into the arena while the stands are full of critics (including yourself).

Steve Jobs said, "Real artists ship!"

You need to be brave enough to try something new. And only once you have tried it, you will see the patterns, in hindsight ... what is working and what is not working. You can do nothing about what happened in the past; and you cannot see the future. You can only be in the now, in the present moment, prototyping your way through it.

Being okay with just being there in the present moment.

Agile trainer

At the same time that my process was running, another training programme was rolled out: the transition to agile methodologies.

Just before I started the workshop with the teams, my sponsor dropped another one-liner saying, "You need to align your work with agile training".

At that stage, I simply ignored it because that was just one step too many for me.

Fortunately, the very organised lady in charge of the project arrangements made an appointment for me with the agile trainer.

The agile trainer introduced me to all the principles and values of the new way of thinking and developing software products. The one thing that stood out for me was this: We prefer responding to change as it happens rather than following a predetermined plan.

It still took me a while to fully understand the impact of this way of thinking and doing, but one of the first pennies that dropped was, "I need to integrate with this philosophy".

Agile cupboard

Back at the boardroom, I told them, "A few of you have already heard my stories and jokes. What do you want to do today?" To my surprise they became co-facilitators, co-creating the workshop as we went along.

"The thing about the personal development cycle really helps me. Please explain it to them too."

"It really helped me to get feedback from my team members. Perhaps we need to do it here as well."

"The appreciative sentence about our team's awareness triggered a new vision for our time."

"After the connection exercises we really connected on a different level."

By that time, I have brought every tool and exercise and poster I have developed to the boardroom and they gave me a cupboard in which to store it. So, when I turned to the cupboard to fetch the exercise we had decided on, I heard one of the members remarking, "Oh, so you have an agile cupboard now!"

Expanding exercise

Describe a time when you really stretched yourself to act differently to what you usually do, and where the end-result surprised you or turned out better than you had expected.

Open to change exercise

Journal about the following three questions:

I participate in life by ...

Complete the sentence with long-term goals, callings and time management decisions.

I choose to risk ...

Complete the sentence with steps you want to take in the direction of your purpose. Include actions that will lead to growth, continuous learning and capacity building.

B Mapping future possibilities – chess is not for anxious souls

"Change your opinions, keep to your principles; change your leaves, keep intact your roots."

– VICTOR HUGO

How can our reading of the now help to form our vision of the future?

Our false future may find it horrifying to change plans and just follow the whims of others. If we do not know what is going to happen, we may resist. We often hold on to what seems certain.

No plan survives contact with the enemy

Helmuth von Moltke (1800-1891) was chief-of-staff of the Prussian army for 30 years. He is regarded as the creator of a modern method of directing armies in the field, and is described as a tactical genius.

His genius lies therein that he did not try to direct his armies through a system of rules. He regarded strategy as the practical art of adapting means to ends.

One of Von Moltke's trademark strategies is called the offensive-defensive strategy. He moved his army to cut the lines of communication of the enemy force and then dig in and defeat the enemy by trying to re-establish its lines of communication in a defensive action.

He understood that in order to make a large army manageable, it should be broken up into separate groups of corps, each group under a commander authorised to regulate its movements and actions subject to the purpose of its operations.

Von Moltke also realised that subordinates would have to use initiative and independent judgement for the forces to be effective in battle. Therefore, overall campaign and battle plans should encourage decentralisation. He accomplished this by means of directives stating his intentions, rather than detailed orders. He was willing to accept deviations from a directive provided it was within the general framework of the mission.

Von Moltke's main thesis was that military strategy had to be understood as a system of options since it was only possible to plan the beginning of a military operation. His ideas can be summed up by two statements:

- "No plan survives contact with the enemy", and
- "Strategy is a system of expedients".

After the war, he became a national hero and celebrity. In the late 19th and early 20th centuries, more than 50 monuments were erected throughout Germany in honour of Von Moltke. Some were destroyed during or after World War II but many have remained to this day. His 90th birthday on 26 October 1890 was declared a national holiday.

As a side note, Patrick Feaster explained that Helmuth von Moltke was born in 1800, technically the last year of the 18th century. In 1889, Moltke made two audio recordings on Thomas Edison's newly invented cylinder phonograph. He recorded excerpts from Shakespeare and Goethe on two cylinders. These recordings were lost until 1957 and unidentified for several decades. In 2012 they were found among a number of recordings revealed by the Thomas Edison National Historical Park.

Patrick Feaster commented, "There's a wonderful irony here. Moltke's nickname was 'der große Schweiger' (the great silent one), because he had a reputation for speaking very little; and yet, of all the hundreds of millions of people born in the 18th century, his is the only voice we can hear today".

Planning the unplannable

The Jewish researchers Nurit Alfasi and Juval Portugali make the distinction between *just-in-case planning* and *just-in-time planning*.

The first refers to the traditional mode of planning. Some people call it Fordism, after the mechanised mass-production methods pioneered by Henry Ford (1863-1947). This type of approach sees life as a machine that has to be planned in detail. The planning must be comprehensive and should precede any attempt to meet the future. You must have a tight grip on life to pre-plan it.

You think of life as a production line where everything is broken up into little steps you must follow. If you simply complete all the tasks, you will have the product you desire at a specific time, according to your calculations. All your planning is to safeguard you against any slight miscalculations or unexpected failures – just in case.

But ... open, complex systems, like life, do not operate in this way. Life does not play by the rules. The story goes that managers from Toyota invented just-in-time planning while visiting a supermarket in the USA during the late 1940s. They discovered that supermarkets had a huge yet simple and efficient supply system. This system worked in a relatively sophisticated way, with little paperwork or stock. They did not use pre-planned steps for ordering new products and quantities. There were no plans to push products on the shelves. The supermarket was running on a simple "pull" routine. The customers pulled the products from the shelves and the supermarket workers replenished them.

The supermarket had no stockroom, just in case. All the fresh products were delivered to the supermarket exactly when they were required, just in time.

Although just-in-time planning is vulnerable, because of its openness and interrelated nature, it has the advantage of making you flexible to changes around you. It opens up possibilities for quick innovation and decision-making. You can quickly respond to unexpected changes.

Life is a game of chess, not for anxious souls

Have you ever had the feeling that you cannot drive yourself any further, and that there is no way out? You know something's got to give. Your body pops, your mind goes blank and relationships go sour.

If you stop and listen to the wisdom of your body, you will usually get the message. The pounding headache is saying, "I cannot handle the stress and lack of sleep anymore". The aching stomach is saying, "I cannot stomach this relationship anymore". The lower back pain is telling you, "I've lost my power. Get out of this job. I'm a round peg in a square hole and it will not get any better."

Acknowledge that life is difficult

Let go of the illusion that there are people who actually have life under control.

Mary Superwomen has a boy and a girl. Her children are well-mannered and they perform excellently at school. She and her husband still take honeymoon breaks while both pursue fulfilling careers and earn good money.

Delete the picture.

It's an illusion.

It only looks perfect from the outside.

Many years ago someone told me that we always juggle a few things: money, job satisfaction and lifestyle. She reckoned that only once in a blue moon do we strike the jackpot with all three appearing on the screen of your gambling machine at once. Most of the time, one or two would be up on the screen.

Welcome to life!

Pause and appreciate the one or two ups and accept the downs. Or decide to change your position.

It is difficult to make hard decisions. Why? Because it puts us in a position of split loyalties. For example, should I be a good provider or a good father and spend more time with my family? Should I be a good mother and stay at home with my kids, or should I be a good mother by helping to provide so that my kids will have more opportunities? Should I enjoy life as a single person and put all my energy into my career?

Acknowledge the "committee of voices" in your head. We all have a committee operating in our heads. Voices from the present and past tell us what is good and bad. They tell us what to do and what not to do. We know they are there when we need to decide. The voice in our heads says, "Can you really afford to take that long a vacation?" Or the voice might say the following when you want to change jobs for more satisfaction and less income, "This is selfish. You are not thinking of your family!"

Acknowledge the presence of the "committee members" and then politely send them away to where they came from. Only then will you be free to take the next step.

Here's the truth: The risk of not acting is greater than the cost of making the wrong choice. Because when you fail, you learn. When you don't commit, you don't act. Nothing happens. When you pause, and stall, you don't learn. Even wrong choices help you grow and make you stronger. As Jeff Going says, "Failure is a friend dressed up like an enemy".

C Calm regardless of what is coming my way

"If you treat problems as possibilities, life will start to dance with you in the most amazing ways."

– MARTIN VILLENEUVE, FILMMAKER

How can we calmly receive the future that is unfolding?

Brian Millar tells of a newspaper article about a missing woman. A group of tourists spent hours looking for a woman near Iceland's Eldgjá canyon. The group was on a tour bus and stopped near the volcanic canyon. Soon there was word of a missing passenger. The woman, who had changed clothes, did not realise they talked about her, and joined in the search. The search was called off at three in the morning when it became clear the missing woman was, in fact, accounted for and searching for herself.

Brain commented, "Aren't we all, in our own way, this woman?"

Our false future can be indifferent and powerless in terms of everything that is happening to it. We can become almost invisible in our own show.

How to become a shapeshifter

"Life is a series of natural and spontaneous changes. Don't resist them; that only creates sorrow. Let reality be reality. Let things flow naturally forward in whatever way they like."

– LAO TZU

This week, you are developing a secret power: shapeshifting. You are learning how to cut through life like a hot knife through butter. Morphing into who you want to be. Gracefully rising above challenges, fluidly overcoming setbacks.

As a shapeshifter, I do not function based on fixed perceptions. I know I choose my perceptions. I co-create my reality. The outside is simply a projection from within. I notice what I pay attention to. How I then interpret what I have noticed makes all the difference. Shapeshifting is ascribing new meaning and interpretation to my perceptions of what is coming towards me.

Think of something that is coming your way from the future. It can be something you fear or something you desire. Use the list of questions below to shift the meaning you are attaching to this coming event.

Shift from negative towards potential:

- What's good about this situation?
- What can I learn from this person or situation?
- How is this experience changing me in a good way?
- What's the gift in this situation?

Shift from victim towards taking charge:

- How did I create this?
- What is this situation an example of?
- Where else in my life am I creating this issue?
- What can I change in me that will change 'their' behaviour?

Shift from inward looking towards outside perspective:

- If I was coaching someone with this issue what would I say to them?
- How would I feel if this situation did not involve me? What changes would occur within me?
- How is the other person feeling right now?
- If I was experiencing this in a movie, what would I notice as I watch myself?

Shift from specific towards the bigger picture:

- What is this an example of?
- What do we both have in common?
- For what purpose is this happening to me?
- Why is this important to me?

Shift from monkey chatter towards creativity:

- Did I encounter something unusual in my day-to-day routine? How is this a metaphor of me and my life?
- If this is a metaphor, how does it reframe my current thinking?
- What is this fresh insight doing to old wounds that tend to rise to the surface? How does it heal me?
- Why is this significant? What meaning could this experience/situation hold for me personally?

Examples of metaphors: Someone mentioned several times, something you use regularly that goes wrong, an animal encounter, traffic jams, delays, numbers, certain words or pictures, a song or phrase you keep hearing, and pain or sensations in your body.

Shift from ordinary to out of the ordinary:

- Did I experience something unusual or 'out of the ordinary'? What was my initial response that came up from my intuition?
- How does this relate to other aspects of my life?
- What am I learning at this stage in my life, assuming that everyone I meet has an interesting insight from which I can learn?
- How can I open up my vision to embrace the unseen on a moment-by-moment basis?

As Nikki J Owen said: "The way you look at your life, the way you look at others, the way you perceive your issues and challenges is directly linked to the joy and wonder you feel. You have the power to shift the shape of every problem, every challenge and every difficulty. You have the power to find the gift in every issue you encounter. When you accept that you are a Shapeshifter then you begin to exercise your ability to transform the seemingly mundane into an extraordinary opportunity."

Do something new today

When you do something new, it gives you a new perspective. Doing new things helps you to learn. It makes you nimble. Having a wide range of experiences of unconventional situations primes you for innovation. It inspires you to move beyond the blocks on the board. Doing new things stretches you. Doing unfamiliar tasks will vitalise your brain.

Task: Ask why questions

- If you often think about *your capacity to react to change,* ask yourself: Why am I always busy with something new?
- If you almost never think about *your capacity to react to change,* ask yourself: Why don't I care about what's coming at me?

Reflection: Checking in on my future

- How often did you manage to do your journaling?
- Can you think of a successful transition in your life? What were your insights? If not, take a moment to identify a possible transformation.
- Which one of the shapeshifters did you identify with? Why?
- What did you struggle with?
- What are you discovering about your ability to adapt to change?

For the more adventurous

- **Draw outside »** Working in open air can be a fun way to relax and get in touch with nature while you are working on a piece of art. Let yourself be free. Don't allow yourself to judge your work. If you think your paintings are too tight and controlled, try a looser style. Paint to music. Letting your creativity flow in response to music is a great way to let out feelings and just relax.
- **Dream-catcher »** Make a dream-catcher. Having bad dreams? Create this age-old tool to catch your dreams. Or draw your dreams. You can learn a lot from what goes on in your dreams. So, keep a dream journal and use it for inspiration to draw or paint.
- **Scribble drawing »** With this activity you can turn a simple scribble into something beautiful, using lines, colour and your creativity.
- **Mountains and valleys »** Paint or draw a mountain and a valley. The mountain can represent a time when you were happy; the valley can represent a time when you were sad. Also add elements that reflect specific events.

TEN
Recognising the full worth of my collaboration

I know fully where we stand with each other.

Values – the influence I let others have

This week explores the influence you allow others to have on you. The readings and tools in this book are aimed at guiding you to see yourself living with others around the "village fountain". You navigate between not being allowed to participate and not being able to provide input. You will discover that you are trying to get people to do what you know is best for them, or that you are entering into agreements with them in order to form a reliable group. The aim of this week is to get to a space where you give people space and trust them to do the right thing.

"It is the long history of humankind (and animal kind, too) that those who learned to collaborate and improvise most effectively have prevailed."
– CHARLES DARWIN

I know fully where we stand with each other.

I provide direction.
I am the anchor at the core of the team.
I know trust is better than control.

What to expect this week: Tempted onto side roads

Rather than a smooth journey home, Week 10 confronts you with new and unexpected challenges on your journey of embracing your authentic self. You are tempted to go down side roads. You need to rededicate yourself to your original quest.

Now is the time to complete the journey. You are more than three-quarters of the way. You will practise to leave the time of transformation behind and to bring what you have learnt back home. You have discovered a treasure that quickly needs to be brought back to your "old world". Feel the sense of urgency you have. Be vigilant of dangers on your road back home. Be aware of what you need to denounce to live authentically. Start slowing down.

If this 12-week journey was a movie, you would enter the chase scene this week. You are driving as fast as you can, the whole time on the brink of losing what you seek. As things are becoming clearer, the urgency is increasing. The danger is growing. Everything seems to be happening at the same time. You are urged to act in an instant.

This stage in Little Hans's journey represents a reverse echo of the adventure on which he has been the past few weeks. Now he must return home with his reward. This time, the expectation of danger is replaced with that of celebration and perhaps freedom or even release.

But Little Hans's journey is not over yet. He may still need one last push back into the real world. The moment before he finally commits to the last stage of his journey may be a moment in which he must choose between his own personal objective and that of a cause greater than himself.

My authentic collaboration

My authentic collaboration has natural delegation powers. I create space for everyone to do what they need to do but within a larger context of doing things together.

I can and want to work without someone watching over my shoulder. It is about giving people space and trusting them to do the right thing.

I have the ability to trust people with what they do.

My authentic collaboration exudes trust. Hence, very few people feel the need to control me. Similarly, I will very seldom reprimand others. I know that the optimal development of people happens when they are allowed to apply their own strengths and set their own goals.

I can, therefore, delegate well and appreciate the value of others.

A Take control – provide direction

"Criticism, like rain, should be gentle enough to nourish a man's growth without destroying his roots."

– FRANK A. CLARK

Your question this week is: How can I convince people to do what I know is best for them?

Your false collaboration can only know one side of the truth – your truth. You set yourself up against every other opinion or decision but are uncomfortable when others handle you in the same way.

However, there is another way of leading. This comes out of an adult mindset.

When the situation calls for it, you can use your natural delegation power. This will create space for everyone to do what they need to do. You will be able to convince them to do things together. Your leadership will create guarded space were people are trusted to do the right thing.

You remember that the most favourable development of people happens when they are allowed to commit to their own strengths and set their own goals.

Staying in an adult mindset

The function of an adult mindset is to seek and give out information, analyse data, make decisions and take responsibility. It is not impulsive. When you are in an adult mindset you talk in factual terms and tend to be unemotional. An adult mindset has a sense of humour and is the best evaluator of reality.

When you are functioning from your adult mindset and the other person involved is tending to do otherwise, there are a number of things you can do to help keep the exchange on an adult-to-adult basis.

Read through the following list and decide what you can do this week to stay in an adult mindset.

1. **Ask questions that will open up the discussion.**
    - What else can you tell me about this?
    - What other angle is there?
    - What kind of reaction have you had?

2. **Ask for clarification.**
    - Could you explain that point again?
    - Exactly who was responsible?
    - Is this what you mean?

3. **Check out the facts.**
    - Are those the correct figures?
    - What is the source of your information?
    - What date was this issued?

4. **Acknowledge and empathise with the other person's feelings.**
    - I can see this has upset you.
    - You're obviously concerned, and I can understand why.
    - You have put a lot into this and you seem to be feeling undervalued.

5. **Listen attentively.**
   - Signal your attention with your body language.
   - Show sympathy in your facial expression.
   - Allow pauses for thinking and re-phrasing.

6. **Admit mistakes openly.**
   - You're quite right — I made an error here in the second column.
   - I know I was wrong about the timing of that.
   - It was delivered to the wrong customer. My mistake entirely.

7. **Leave the door to negotiation open.**
   - Perhaps there's another option.
   - Perhaps we could look at that next time.
   - Let's think about a new approach.

Leadership manifesto

You know that you have all the inner authority you need to start leading others towards the future. You can start today by creating stories of change and innovation and by being remarkable. Read the following leadership manifesto. Which one of these slogans do you want to take up as a personal battle cry?

This manifesto was inspired by Seth Godin's book *Tribes: We Need You to Lead Us* (2008). When you have read through all the slogans, write down a few that you would like to make your own.

As a leader I will let go of the status quo because I believe in a new world and new community ...

- I will lead my team to be remarkable.
- I will lead others to create things of value that energise and transform our generation.
- I will be generous and not concerned about getting credit for what I did.
- I will be authentic and spend my time and energy on things I believe in.
- I will face my fears to challenge the status quo and change the world.
- I will unmask the illusion of stability and I will take a step forward.
- I will amplify the achievements of the people around me.
- I will stop fighting change and studying everything to death.
- I will stand up in front of strangers, propose ideas and resist the urge to blend in.
- I will be curious and teachable because I know the real innovation will come out of the blue and will not be managed.
- I will stop waiting for things to happen and start making things happen.
- I will colour over the lines and do amazing stuff.
- I will seek, embrace and reward innovation.
- I will face my fear of being wrong and stop criticising people who actually take risks.
- I will paint pictures of the future.
- I will listen and lead because I believe that leadership can come from anyone, from anywhere and from any distance.

- I will create platforms where ideas that work can spread.
- I will create a culture of gracious and honest communication around the dreams we pursue.
- I will stop striving for perfection (and just do the things I do better).
- I will change the rules and raise the bar.
- I know I have all the authority.
- I need to take a position and innovate.
- I believe it is more fun to make rules than to follow them.
- I will start doing this today.
- I will not do nothing!
- I will lead!

B Anchors at the core of the team

> *"No one can whistle a symphony. It takes a whole orchestra to play it."*
> – H.E. LUCCOCK

How can we make agreements with everyone in order to form a reliable group?

We value equality, and members have the power to push back.

Our false collaboration can regard appointments as cast in stone. This rigidity often does not allow any flexibility. This can push us out of the game in teamwork and collaboration.

Validation: the speed-dial solution to restore relationships

When you talk to someone and the heat goes up and you do not have plenty of time to get the issue resolved, there is a magic speed dial to get to a solution.

When there is a difference in opinion or when someone takes criticism badly (like most of us), or when you push someone's "buttons", the other person goes into a fight or flight mode. That worked quite well in the days of the cave men and women, who often found themselves in life-threatening situations. The adrenaline drug came in very useful to strengthen their bodies. These days, we still experience this urge when we are upset. However, in our "civilised" world we need to sit or stand still and keep on talking as if nothing has happened.

I learned about validation from Harville Hendrix. He developed what he calls Imago Therapy. Validation is a response to the other person that his or her information has been received and that it makes sense. In other words, you are not mad – every person's biggest fear.

There are three different ways of validating:

1. **Flat mirror validation**

   This means you give a clear indication that you understand the other person's point of view and the thinking process or argument behind his or her words. You understand and respect it, without necessarily agreeing with it. You understand that it makes sense to the other person, without adding any interpretation or correction of the view point (flat mirror). Phrase that work well are:

   "What you are saying makes sense because …"

   "I can see that …"

   "You make sense to me because …"

   "I can understand that …"

   Such phrases convey to the other person that his or her subjective experience has its own logic and is a valid way of looking at things.

2. **Power validation**

   You use power validation in heated or conflict situations when you were partly responsible for upsetting the other person. You need to be brave enough to own your contribution that added to the other person's frustration or caused the conflict by adding it to the validation statement. Here are a few examples:

   "You make sense when you say that you feel under pressure and undervalued because I did not always recognise your hard work in person."

   "You make sense when you're saying that you're frustrated about all the changes in the company because we did, in fact, make changes, knowing that you could feel uncomfortable with them."

   "You make sense when you're saying that you do not trust me anymore because I made the decision not to communicate certain information about the company to you."

   When you can claim your part in something, you are making a very powerful validation of the other person's experiences. Although this is difficult to do, it goes a long way in bringing people together. Often this kind of support for the other person will bring immediate results and you will see it on his or her face when you claim your part in an issue.

3. **Appreciative validation**

   You use appreciative validation when you want to empower and strengthen people's positive behaviour. In fact, when you want to change a person's behaviour, the best way to do this is by reinforcing their positive behaviour.

   Again, validate the thinking but also the impact of what the person did in a very specific and concrete way. It still needs to be true, otherwise the statement would lose its credibility and cause more harm and distrust.

   Here is the recipe: Firstly, describe the behaviour. Secondly, say how it made you feel. Thirdly, explain the effect that this behaviour has had on you and on the team or process you are working on. Here are some examples:

"When you completed the report in two days instead of the required week, we as a team were delighted because we could then carry on completing the full report for the management meeting and hand it in prior to the deadline. We were complimented on our efficiency during the meeting."

"Yesterday, when you made an effort to come home early to help me with the kids, I felt relieved and cared for. This made it possible for me to carry on with supper, and we as a family could have a happy meal together."

C Trust is better than control

> *"A team is not a group of people who work together. A team is a group of people who trust each other."*
> — SIMON SINEK

Don't take it personally

The question you are thinking about now is: How can I give people space and trust them to do the right thing?

Your false collaboration may retreat behind a glass wall of "I am unapproachable". This may leave others in the dark about what they want and what they do. This can make others feel as if they are left to their own devices.

In his book *The Four Agreements: A Practical Guide to Personal Freedom,* Don Miguel Ruiz proposes this agreement: Don't take anything personally.

He makes the argument, "Nothing other people do is because of you. It is because of them." Other people live in a completely different world than you. When we take something personally, we make the assumption that they know what is going on in our world. We also try to impose our world on their world. Even if it feels personal, it has nothing to do with you. Even if the insult is direct, it is still their stuff. What they say and do comes out of the ideas in their minds. We can stop treating other people's emotional garbage. When we stop taking it personally, we become immune in the middle of hell.

Rather than feeling offended, don't take it personally.

Rather than defending your beliefs, don't take it personally.

Rather than making something big out of it, don't take it personally.

Rather than needing to be right, don't take it personally.

Rather than trying hard to give your own opinion, don't take it personally.

Whatever others think or feel is their problem and not your problem. It is the way they see the world. It is not personal. It has nothing to do with you.

Make the following agreement with yourself: Whatever other people do, feel, think or say, I won't take it personally.

Task: Ask why questions

- If you often think about the influence you let others have, ask yourself: Why do I like to do things together with others?
- If you almost never think about the influence you let others have, ask yourself: Why do I prefer doing things without others?

Reflection: Checking in on my collaboration

- How often did you manage to do your journaling?
- How did "staying in the adult mindset" assist you this week?
- Reflect on where you could use "Don't take it personally".
- What did you struggle with?
- What are you discovering about the way in which you collaborate?

For the more adventurous

- **Coat of arms** » Choose symbols that represent your strengths and create your own special coat of arms.
- **Expressive website** » A website is a very versatile way to express yourself. Build your own website to express what is most important to you.
- **Perfect day** » Think about what constitutes a perfect day for you. Then make a collage of your vision of a perfect day. What part of this collage can you turn into a reality today? Take photographs of how you think things should be and how people should interact. No one else has to like them, only you. Print and frame them to have constant reminders of how you think life should be lived.
- **Box of values** » Create a box of values. First, collage or paint a box that represents you. Then place items in the box that represent the things you value the most.

ELEVEN
Recognising the full worth of my outside

I show who I am.

Ambition – my mask towards the other

This week may find you grappling with the mask you show. This means it is time look at the face you put on for others. Maybe you feel that you are not seen or do not know what others expect of you. You will explore what you do, or do not do, to make others see what you can bring. You will also consider ways to discover what others expect of you and how you can show those qualities. The aim of this week is to embody invitation that puts people at ease, making them feel welcome.

> *"Be yourself; everyone else is already taken."*
> – OSCAR WILDE

I show who I am.
My enthusiasm brings movement.
I am determined to show the best.
I embody invitation.

What to expect this week: Struggling to stay authentic

Week 11 sees you struggling with a final attempt. There is a final challenge you must survive to integrate your authentic self into your new life. This week you will once more be severely tested at the threshold of home. You were stripped and purified by your journey, and now there is one last moment of death and rebirth – this time on a higher and more complete level. All that will remain is your authentic self. Based on what you choose to do, the polarities that were in conflict at the beginning of your journey will finally be resolved. You will be transformed. You will be a changed person. You will enter your new life.

This is the climax in which Little Hans will have his final and most dangerous encounter with death. The final battle also represents something far greater than his own existence. Its outcome will have far-reaching consequences for his world and the lives of those he left behind.

If he fails, others will suffer. This places more weight upon his shoulders. All his hopes and fears depend on this final attempt. Ultimately, Little Hans succeeds. He destroys his enemy and emerges from the battle reborn.

Meet your trickster

Part of your journey to authenticity is being cut down to size; having a mirror held up before you to confront you with your own ego, arrogance and false ideas about yourself. This often comes in the way of a trickster. Tricksters are full of mischief energy and the desire to invite change. They are typically clowns or comical sidekicks. They will often toy with you. They will force you to confront your true nature.

Your last inner process is to destroy any big ego that is left. You will also be confronted by any remaining foolish and hypocritical aspects.

Who around you are helping you to grow through self-examination, laughter and humility? They are the tricksters in your life. They often provide comic relief. They also relieve tension, suspense and conflict.

My authentic outside

Read the following description of your authentic outside. Become aware of how much of this is true of you at this moment. How much of it is a deep longing you have? What emotions are awakened by this description? What do you need to let go of in order to become your authentic outside?

My outside embodies invitation. I show my most endearing smiles to the world. I am quick to put people at ease with my kindness.

I want to be perceived as inviting and open. My friendliness and ability to listen makes everyone feel welcome.

My outside is inviting, friendly, open and receiving. I know how to make people feel welcome. I want others to know that they can always ask me for help and that I am always there for them. That is why I am well-loved and why people feel safe with me.

I ask the right kind-hearted questions and give the correct answers calmly. I know how to put people at ease without interfering too much. I am present without being overwhelming. However, I rarely go unnoticed and I am always pleasantly visible.

Write down in your journal what happened to you while you were reading this.

Challenges and obstacles

Your intuitive self will urge you to become attention seeking. Your false outside will fail to see the boundaries of others. You will constantly want to show others what you found or who you are. You will be overly concerned about not adding value.

This "see me" attitude may also implode in a "please don't notice me" stance. Still anxious about how you will be perceived, you choose to be seen by trying not to be seen.

Ⓐ Enthusiasm brings movement

"You were born to stand out, stop trying to fit in."
– ROY T. BENNETT

Let us spend time on this question: How can I make other people see what I can bring?

Your false outside may also be busy with your interpretation of others' wishes while ignoring your own needs and longings. You then demand more of yourself than others expect of you. You set high expectations for yourself and almost kill yourself trying to achieve them. And just when it seems as if you will succeed, you lift these lofty goals higher still.

Ed Tronick and the "still face experiment"

The still face experiment was undertaken by Edward Tronick in 1978. The experiment starts with a mother happily engaging face to face with an equally happy baby. After some time, she is asked to hold a "still face". During this time she does not react to the baby's behaviour. The reactions of the baby are then observed. In general, the baby will become agitated by failed attempts to evoke a reaction in the mother.

The researchers described their findings as follows, "The infant first orients toward the mother," and "greets her expectantly". But then, when the mother "fails to respond appropriately," the infant "rapidly sobers and grows wary. He makes repeated attempts to get the interaction into its usual reciprocal pattern. When these attempts fail, the infant withdraws and orients his face and body away from his mother with a withdrawn, hopeless facial expression."

The still face experiment is a powerful study that shows our need for connection from very early in life. This experiment gives us insight into what it is like when connection does not occur.

The still face experiment also demonstrates that, from a very young age, we have several basic building blocks of social understanding in place. It suggests that we have a deep sense of the relationship between facial expression and emotion. The infant's attempts to re-engage with the parent suggest that they are able to plan and execute simple behaviours to reconnect.

By repeating the same experiment over the years, researchers have shown how children's social and emotional development becomes richer as they grow older. Their responses become increasingly complex with age. They include deftly timed facial cues, dampened smiles, sideways glances at their parent, and yawns. One researcher tells of an experiment in which a five-month-old boy, upon encountering a still face, stopped being wary and "looked at the mother and laughed briefly. After this brief tense laugh, he paused, looked at her soberly, and then laughed again, loud and long, throwing his head back as he did so. At this point, the mother became unable to maintain an unresponsive still face."

Many parents can relate to this. Armed with a stern face, they try earnestly to reprimand their child, only to be met with a cheeky grin or giggle.

There are two types of questions to ask yourself here:

- Do I sometimes struggle to show my emotions? Do I feel shut down?
- Do I have people in my life who tell me they want to see more of an emotional reaction from me?
- Were there emotions that were unacceptable to show when I was a child?
- Am I so overwhelmed with life that I find it difficult to smile or talk to others?

Or:

- Am I "the child acting out" because it feels as if others don't see me?
- Do I feel agitated because of my failed attempts to evoke a reaction from the people around me?
- Do I often withdraw and orient my face and body away from others with a hopeless facial expression?

Skinny-dipping into life

It is not the critic who counts; not the man who points out how the strong man stumbles, or where the doer of deeds could have done them better. The credit belongs to the man who is actually in the arena, whose face is marred by dust and sweat and blood; who strives valiantly; ... who at best knows in the end the triumph of high achievement, and who at worst, if he fails, at least fails while daring greatly.

- THEODORE ROOSEVELT

Not so long ago, I was facilitating a four-day workshop in Johannesburg, South Africa's largest city. It was just before lunch on the last day, and I was closing the workshop with a motivational video. While debriefing the video, one of the participants, an academic trainer, started protesting. She still did not have enough knowledge. She lacked the skills to go out and put into practice what we have learnt. Her fellow participants came to her rescue. They validated her skills and knowledge. They encouraged her to go out and start doing what I had taught them. The more they cheered her on, the more she protested. In a very eloquent and academic way, she stated why she was not ready yet. She claimed it would be unprofessional and risky to storm out and use this new knowledge, especially in the academic environment in which she was working.

I got that sinking feeling – that feeling most trainers and facilitators know so well. It is that dreadful feeling you experience when, on the last day of a workshop that forms part of an intervention you have facilitated with so much passion and effort over a period of six months, you realise that the penny did not drop for everyone!

You need a lot of the self-awareness that you are so consciously cultivating not to drop your mask and tell the participant how attention seeking this is. Or how bad you feel about yourself for not being able to empower and enable her to go out and do what she was taught to do. Or how selfish it was of her not to understand what this is doing to you and the rest of the group.

Earlier that same day, I showed the group at the workshop in Johannesburg Brené Brown's video based on Theodore Roosevelt's quote about "the man in the arena". I was introduced to the work of Brown and her book *Daring Greatly* when managing a big project for an IT company in Cape Town in 2014. Since then I have read the book and watched numerous of her YouTube videos.

In this video, Brown unpacks the metaphor of the man in the arena trying his best in the sweat and blood and dust, while the critics watch from the cheap seats and comment on everything. Her advice eventually is not to listen to any critic or anyone who is not down there in the arena sweating with you. You need only a handful of people that care and love you despite your imperfections. These are the people who can affirm, "Yes, this was horrible," but who will then pick you up, dust you off and send you back in.

You also have to become vulnerable to get up from where you are sitting in front of the stairs while you are "ordering fast food and having a picnic", postponing climbing the stairs and showing up. This is where you armour yourself with excuses and where you listen to the critics or gremlins in your head telling you that you are not good enough, that you do not know enough, that you are not smart enough, and that you are not ready to show up. Again, vulnerability is needed to stand up and start climbing the stairs. Explaining this in the video, Brown said, "Get naked ... and go in there!"

So, the next moment I heard myself saying to the workshop participant, "We had a ball camping out for five weekends while doing this workshop. I am not prepared to eat another pizza with you camping out. Because I care enough, I am going to push you into the arena ... Get naked ... and go in there!" Everyone cheered and we could see how she changed gears. Her face lighting up, she asked, "May I wear my pink polka dot bikini?"

Pandemonium broke loose in the class as every woman, most of them aged around 40 or 50 years, including the woman who protested, imagined ourselves in pink polka dot bikinis. All of a sudden everyone was volunteering vulnerable and suitable non-armour costumes for the arena. It varied from tutus to belly-dancing costumes.

This is where we as a group decided that humour helps a lot with vulnerability. We decided to wear just enough to still go in naked (with a smile) and skinny dip into life.

The next day she posted on our message group that she wants to celebrate with us the fact that she did her first awareness feedback session, with her boss of all people, and that it had been a wonderful experience.

B Determined to show the best

"You're the only you. So if you want to be original, just be yourself."

– MARTY RUBIN

Your disconnected false outside may be so out of touch with yourself that you cannot make contact with others. Your smiles can be unsettling. People can be unsure how to handle you and start avoiding you.

The question to ponder is this: How can I know what others expect of me and show the corresponding skills and qualities in me?

Not being good enough

I once facilitated an awareness journey for a client: In front of me was a well-groomed, friendly and professional woman. Later I heard she had just arrived back from maternity leave. There was no sign that she recently gave birth to a baby. She appeared to be in perfect shape.

When she started talking, she criticised herself for not exercising enough, for not finding balance between home and work, and for being detail-oriented enough. She carried on with this self-criticism.

It seemed as if she had everything under control. Yet, she had this internal struggle with not being good enough. It's not as if I don't know this monster called "not-being-good-enough". Somehow, I just struggled to go beyond her perfect appearance to see and empathise with this "monster".

So I smiled politely and started giving her feedback from the assessment she had completed. However, with every personal strength I explained to her, she immediately verbalised the shadow.

Let me pause here for a moment. I started typing up Gillian's story. I tried my best but really struggled. I was stuck. Feeling pretentious, I decided to go to bed.

The next morning I told Nico that I had started with Gillian's story, and about the fact that she would always try to show the right emotions. I knew this story had a beautiful ending, but I could not get into the flow of it.

While I was talking, I got it! *She* was looking over *my* shoulder. *She* was checking whether *I* remembered the story correctly. *She* was critically checking if *I* was putting in too much detail or too little. I was wondering if she would approve of the story and let me use it in the book. I was wondering if I was writing it correctly.

It was a relief to understand my own feelings of not being good enough. This insight unblocked my flow! I immediately started to write again.

Then another insight dawned on me. I know this monster called not-being-good-enough so intimately that it tuned in with hers. I saw she conquered hers, but mine was still alive and well.

I think this is what we are trying to do in *Going Meta*. Writing about awareness made me become aware of my own awareness. Thank you, Gillian, for this gift.

Some 18 months after we started Gillian's awareness journey, we were sitting in a coffee shop for our follow-up. We both decided we needed a more informal setting. It was more as if we were friends meeting to reflect on our journey together. The woman in front of me was still friendly and even more beautiful. We were chatting and connecting on what had happened in our lives since we last met.

She started explaining how I pushed her to embrace her strategy as gifts and not as the perceived negative shadows. She recalled how hard it was, but when she broke through, it was so liberating. She recalled how she formed a new identity, embracing her gifts as part of who she is.

In the meantime, the company she was working for decided to shift the development team out of the country and she needed to find a new job. She remarked, "In the past, I would wonder whether I was good enough, but now I know who I am. In the interviews, it is as if I am interviewing the company to check whether *they* will support who I am, and not the other way round. I am so proud of myself that I am not just taking any job."

C Embodying invitation

"Vulnerability is not winning or losing; it's having the courage to show up and be seen when we have no control over the outcome. Vulnerability is not weakness; it's our greatest measure of courage."

– BRENÉ BROWN

Let us spend time on this question: How can I embody invitation to put people at ease and make them feel welcome?

Embody invitation, put people at ease and smile

A writer on ethics was once asked how to respond when your neighbour brings you food that is inedible. Is it acceptable to lie? He explained that one has three options. The first is to say that the food was horrible: "The food tasted awful." The second is to be vague:" I have never tasted something like this." The third is to say how nice the food was: "We really enjoyed it." Then he added: "In this situation, the commandment to be kind is greater than the commandment to be truthful." To be kind is often the "commandment".

In his 1936 bestselling book *How to Win Friends and Influence People*, Dale Carnegie's second rule to get people to like you is: SMILE. Carnegie was an American writer and lecturer, and the developer of courses in self-improvement, public speaking and interpersonal skills. One of the core ideas in his books is that it is possible to change other people's reactions towards you by changing your behaviour toward them. He quotes a (supposedly) Chinese proverb: "A man without a smiling face must not open a shop." The message is this: If you want to be more approachable, smile.

Professor Richard Wiseman, in his book *59 Seconds* (2009), argued the same point. He stated that we think sad people cry and happy people smile. But this process also works in reverse. If you behave in a certain way, you will feel certain emotions. To test this researchers took two sets of people and asked them to judge how funny they found a set of cartoons. One group was asked to hold a pencil between their teeth, ensuring that it did not touch their lips. The other group supported the end of the pencil with their lips but not their teeth. Wiseman explains: "Without realizing it, those in the 'teeth only' condition had forced the lower part of their faces into a smile, while those in the 'lips only' condition had made themselves frown." (Try it, I know you want to.) The results reveal that those participants who had their faces forced into a smile found the cartoons much funnier than those who were forced to frown.

The second message is clear: If you want to be happier, behave like a happy person and SMILE.

Fogging

Fogging is a technique that functions as a mask to handle micro-aggressions, unfair criticism and rudeness. It may be used when someone makes a remark to hurt you. It is useful when someone's actions is like a personal attack on you or when the remark is entirely untrue.

It can also be used to cope with unasked-for criticism or aggressive manipulation. So, we can use fogging instead of displaying defensive reactions.

How does fogging work? Rather than arguing back, it aims to give a minimal and calm response. You use terms that are calming but not defensive, while at the same time not agreeing to meet demands.

Fogging involves agreeing with any truth that may be contained within statements, even if critical, by – and here the trusting mask comes into play – not responding in the expected way. In other words, by not responding in a defensive or argumentative way. This forces the other person to cease the confrontation as the desired effect is not being achieved. When the atmosphere is less heated, it will be possible to discuss the issues more reasonably. This is called fogging because you act like a "wall of fog" into which arguments are thrown but not returned.

It is, however, important to understand that this technique should only be used if the relationship is not that important to you. Do not use it in intimate relationships because it will block communication and disarm the other person.

How to use fogging

Do not agree or disagree with or ignore the other person. Answer the person in a vague manner. Do not act defensively or emotionally, and do not make excuses for yourself.

The different types of fogging include the following:

Agree with the truth » Here is an example: "You are wearing that ugly shirt again." Say, "Yes, I'm wearing it again" instead of, "What is wrong with my shirt?"

Agree with the logic » Here is an example: "If we had bought a new car instead of keeping this old piece of junk, we would never have had to pay for all the repairs!" Say, "Yes, these high maintenance costs were not necessary," instead of, "Money! Money! Money! That's all you think about. Why don't you just stop?"

Leave space for improvement » Here is an example: "Your work is exceptionally untidy!" Say, "I'm sure that it can be neater."

Recognise the other person's opinion » Here is an example: "You are the slowest worker here in comparison to everybody else." Say, "You are entitled to your opinion. Perhaps I am the slowest worker."

Task: Ask why questions

- If you think a lot about your mask towards the other ask yourself: Why do I always want attention?
- If you almost never think about your mask towards the other ask yourself: Why do I always want to hide?

Reflection: Checking in on my outside

- How often did you manage to do your journaling?
- What symbolises your final challenge on this journey? What can you celebrate so far?
- How are you different, or how do you "stand out" in life?
- What did you struggle with?
- What are you discovering about what you want to show on the outside?

For the more adventurous

- **Expressive self-portrait »** Paint in expressive colours. Select colours for emotional impact. Think about yourself as a strong, capable person by drawing yourself as a warrior.

- **Multi-sided portrait** » Draw the different sides of yourself. In this project, you will explore the different aspects of your personality, giving each a visual representation.
- **Face collage** » We all wear masks of some sort. Create a face collage on a mask. This project lets you showcase your masks and the face you put on for the world.
- **Bag portrait** » Draw a bag self-portrait. On the outside of a paper bag, create a self-portrait. On the inside, fill it with things that represent who you are.
- **Painted window** » Windows let you see inside or outside. Paint your window with things you want to hide from the world or show to the world.
- **Perfect sculpture** » Sculpt your ideal self. If you could make yourself into the perfect person, what would you look like?

TWELVE
Recognising the full worth of my origin

I recognise my line of descent in who I am.

Norms – the intangible influences from out there

This week, you will become aware of the intangible influences from out there. You will explore the large "net" that both supports and controls you. It may be difficult as well as exciting to see how you can challenge the obstacles you face. You will face your fear of being pushed out, or feelings of not having roots that support your being. You will discover how to live as an example of decent conduct. The invitation is to be rooted in yourself and to live the life you were meant to live.

"You will finally have dignity when you realize that you are not on the path, but have become the path for others."
– SHANNON L. ALDER

I recognise my line of descent in who I am.

I bend things that are seen as straight lines.
I am the first among equals.
I stand for eternal truth.

What to expect this week: Returning home a changed person

Week 12 is all about embracing what you have mastered during the past 12 weeks. You will be returning home a changed person. Of course, this is an ongoing journey but you will be travelling on this new road bearing the fruits of your adventure.

On your quest, you received a treasure that has the power to transform the world as you have been transformed. This week you will start living again, but this time as a transformed person. For you there is a new status quo, a new world, a new life. Everything is the same but everything has also changed.

This is the final stage of Little Hans's journey in which he returns home to his world a changed man. He has grown as a person. He has learned many things. He has faced many dangers and even death. Now he looks forward to the start of a new life. His return may bring fresh hope to those he left behind. It may be a direct solution to their problems, or perhaps a new perspective for everyone to consider.

The final reward that Little Hans will obtain may be literal or symbolic. It could be a cause for celebration, self-realisation or an end to conflict. Whatever it is, it represents *change* and *success*. Ultimately, Little Hans returns to the place from where he started but things will clearly never be the same again.

Get out of the "check off" game

Your success lies in holding on to the gift this journey has brought you. In his book *The ONE Thing: The Surprising Simple Truth Behind Extraordinary Results* (2013), Gary Keller tells what he discovered by going "as small as I possibly could go". Looking back at his successes and failures, he noticed an interesting pattern. "Where I reached huge success, I narrowed my concentration to one thing, and where my success varied, my focus had too."

The answer to authentic living is to get to the heart of who you are. It is about "going small".

"Going small" ignores everything you could do and focuses on what you should do. Extraordinary results are directly determined by how narrow you can make your focus. Big success comes when you do a few things well. Again, in Gary's words, "To-do lists tend to be long; success lists are short. One pulls you in all directions; the other aims you in a specific direction ... If your to-do list contains everything, then it's probably taking you everywhere but where you really want to go."

In this final week, it is important to get out of the "check off" game. Your authentic self does not need to be everything for everyone. You want to do "you". Your new-found insights are there to help you too. You need to embody your own roots. You need to be the life you want to see in the world.

Page back to your notes about your playground. Now is the right time to rearrange your surroundings to eliminate the need for multitasking, monkey-minding, bouncing between activities and task switching. This week, you will plot who you were called to be all along. And you will be invited to translate that into an environment that supports you.

My authentic origin

My authentic origin makes me an example of how to live life through the way I create space to think and play.

My natural attraction makes people follow me on my way.

I create spaces in which to think and play as an example of how to live life. I convince people to follow me on my way. I find it quite natural to attract people.

My authentic origin stands for (aspects of) eternal truth. I am an example of trust in human society. I show people how to act in line with their own inner being and how to get closer to their authentic self. Rooted in my origin, I am the obvious example of "practice what you preach". I serve others as I serve everyone – without attachment and without expectations.

Challenges and obstacles

If your anxiety is getting the better of you on your way to embrace your authentic origin you may start fighting against the windmills of the world. This can make you miserable and powerless. These battles soak up a lot of energy and emotions, and lead to nowhere. It is like throwing your fists in the air, or spending energy the furthest away from your power. Or spending passion in your circle of concern and not in your circle of influence.

Another reaction that could trap you in your false self is clinging to the fixed images that others have of you. This keeps you from discovering your own worth. You can become so trapped in how things should be that there is little space for you to move in a different direction. You could be "playing a role" that no longer fits who you are or who you are meant to be.

Disconnecting from your origin could also leave you so powerless that the distance between you and the world becomes a valley that you cannot cross. Then you will start feeling as if the situation is larger than you can handle.

A Bend things seen as straight lines

"Be careful how you interpret the word; it IS like that."
– ERICK HELLER

The first question for this week is: How can I challenge the obstacles I face?

Grit is our future

Grit in spinach makes it inedible. Grit in an assembly line breaks the process. We go to great lengths to eliminate grit. We abhor grit – the immeasurable little bits that make outcomes unpredictable. We love smoothness. Proven processes are the opposite of grit.

But, says Seth Godin, grit is our future.

"Grit is the unexpected bump, the decision that cannot be changed, the insistence on a vision, or the ethics of a creator … We measure sandpaper and grindstones in terms of grit – their ability to stand up to resistance. Someone with grit will grind down the opposition, stand up in the face of criticism, and constantly do what's right for their art. Mostly, they mess up the machine."

Where do you need to be more gritty?

B First among equals

"I'm planting a tree to teach me to gather strength from my deepest roots."
– ANDREA KOEHLE JONES, *THE WISH TREES*

The second last question you are challenged to answer is this: How can I live as an example of decent conduct?

Mandela Day is celebrated every year on Mandela's birthday. The aim is to inspire a ripple of good deeds throughout the world. The goal is to encourage individuals, communities, governments and non-profit organisations to take one small step towards the larger leap of making a positive imprint.

Halfway through a project at a global company with all its ups and downs, I took a two-week break after my father's death. I returned to the project on Mandela Day. The team had a drive for the day and encouraged everyone to take 67 minutes to do something small but significant towards a positive cause.

I started the day with a check-in coffee with my sponsor. She gave me feedback on what she saw as the positive outcomes of the intervention. She started telling stories about various team members and leaders who were inspired by the intervention and started shifting in a positive direction. She started seeing flow towards the Agile transformation, which made a huge difference in the teams.

She was still giving me feedback when she stopped abruptly, saying, "The other day our project administrator called me and explained that you could not be making any money on this project. She said that we originally contracted with you for a much smaller project, which has now evolved into this large intervention. Your rates stayed the same, but you needed to sub-contract with some of your affiliates. This resulted in higher costs to you."

I explained that the rates were agreed upon. I discovered that I had underquoted but that was my problem and part of the "school fees" I was paying.

She shifted in her chair and explained in her "mayor-of-the-project" voice: "Let me tell you how Agile values work. When you start developing a new product or mapping out a process, you can only see and know what you can see and know now. Then you start prototyping or doing stuff in a specific direction from this knowing and insight. Most of the time, the moment you start with the real thing, new insights and knowledge evolve. Then you pause and reflect. With this new knowledge, you pivot or change to fit the circumstances. So we started small with one team. It has now grown to 15 teams and you brought two other people on board. Most of all, this is helping people with the transition. So please re-work your proposal with a realistic rate before the end of the month. It must be sustainable and a win-win for both of us."

I walked away touched by her passionate, caring and fair stance – relieved that I would be able to also pay my affiliates a fair rate and continue with this rewarding project. I was touched by the fact that I am living in South Africa with Mandela as part of our roots. We can follow in his footsteps by being kind and respectful to each other. Most of all, we can follow in his footsteps by being fair and robust in the way we empower people.

I have a dream

Paint a vision of the world.

I want to live in a world where ...

- What would be different?
- What would be better?
- What would be easier?

This is your "I have a dream" speech.

"I want to live in a world where girls at risk have a way out – and up."

"I want to live in a world where meditation is taught in every school."

"I want to live in a world where organic food is super affordable."

Wrap it up by explaining how you are working to create this "better world". Tell us how we can join your revolution.

Here's what I know for sure ...

State what you know. Reveal a few undeniable truths in a poem, an essay or a list.

"This I know: Love is the antidote to fear."

"This I know: One handwritten thank you note can alter the course of someone's day. Or life."

"This I know: When you fall asleep for the last time, you won't wish you'd spent more time linking, tweeting and liking. You'll wish you'd spent more time kissing, laughing and loving."

You can frame this as a letter to your younger self. Or as a collection of truisms for a friend.

Micro-manifesto

If you were at the world's biggest open mic night, and you had only 15 seconds behind the microphone, what would you shout out to the crowd?

"Just dance, baby!"

"Sweat. Stretch. Serve. Smile."

"No one on earth can do what you do, in precisely the way that you do it."

Three statements

Fill out the following three statements:

- I love …
- I believe …
- I am committed to …

I believe …

State what you believe. Use one sentence, a bullet-point list or a whole paragraph.

"I believe in the power of love."

"I believe in real butter and thick-cut bacon."

"I believe that everyone and everything is fascinating – and that everyone has a story worth telling."

Or – for a twist – state what you no longer believe. (And why.)

Focus question

"A people without the knowledge of their past history, origin and culture is like a tree without roots."

– MARCUS GARVEY

Your quest for authentic living is now asking for focus. Reread the answers you gave. Try to stand back. Read them unemotionally. Think back over the previous 12 weeks.

Think of the obstacles you have conquered.

Think of the moments of flow.

From this understanding of, and insights in, the big picture you now need to take the first step.

The following question will help you focus: What is the one thing I can do now that will embody my authentic self?

The big picture is your authentic self. The small focus is the steps in that direction. Each time you step in the direction of your authentic self, the distractions become fewer and the leverage more.

You can only live authentically "right now". There is no tomorrow.

Make a list of all the aspects of your life: your business, job, family, relationships, personal life, health, spiritual life, finances, sports, and so on.

Complete the following sentence for each aspect you listed:

- For my family, what is the one thing I can do today that will embody my authentic self?
- For my job, what is the one thing I can do today that will embody my authentic self?

Now, put down the book and do one of the things you have listed. Until you do that, everything else is a distraction to authentic living.

C Stand for eternal truth

"Continuity gives us roots; change gives us branches, letting us stretch and grow and reach new heights."
– PAULINE R. KEZER

The last question on your quest is this: How can I be my rooted self and live the life I am meant to live?

In his book *The Art of Work: A Proven Path to Discovering What You Were Meant to Do* (2015), Jeff Goins tells of a "dream" conference he attended. He was very aware of the fact that he did not know who he wanted to be or what he wanted to do. It seemed as if everyone had a unique and beautiful dream, except him. Each time he talked about his day job it felt boring and unoriginal. The opening speaker stepped up to the podium and with a few short words "shattered his illusion".

"Some of you here don't know what your dream is. In fact, most of you don't."

Jeff remembered looking around the room and seeing dozens of heads nodding. He did the same, feeling the freedom that comes from admitting he didn't know what he was doing. Then the speaker continued, "But the truth is, you do know what your dream is ... You're just too afraid to admit it."

Jeff wrote, "My heart sank. As soon as he spoke those words, one word popped into my mind: writer. Now I was no longer afraid of failing. I was afraid of not trying."

The One Thing exercise

Gary Keller, author of the book *The ONE Thing: The Surprising Simple Truth Behind Extraordinary Results* (2013), invites you to take the first step towards your authentic self. He invites you to close your eyes and imagine your life as big as it can possibly be.

Do it now. Close your eyes and do the exercise.

Now open your eyes.

Know now that, whatever you saw, you have received the capacity to move towards it. You can grow towards this bigger life you are envisioning. Your authentic origin is the starting point for a bigger life. An authentic life grows out of many generations.

Your roots are encouraging you to live your life fully, without fear. Live with purpose, give it your all, without regrets.

The prospect of change

A journey of discovery presupposes change. For many of us, the idea of reshaping our consciousness is both filled with delight and excitement, and produces fear. The experience of deep change triggers fear of the unknown and the unfamiliar.

People experience the journey to their authentic self in different ways. Ralph Metzner, author of *Ecology of Consciousness: The Alchemy of Personal, Collective, and Planetary Transformation* (2017), made a list of eight classical metaphors for the transformation of human consciousness.

Read through the list and descriptions below. Become aware which of these shifts happened in your life during the past 12 weeks.

1. **From dream-sleeping to awakening**

   Some people experience the discovery of their authentic self as a peeling away of layers or veils. This is accompanied by an increasing sense of greater reality and a heightened vibrancy and clear vision. Everything in your life is less murky or cloudy. The transformation to authenticity occurs when self-perception is altered from illusory self-images to "self-realisation". This awakening comes through more light.

2. **From imprisonment to liberation**

   Authentic living frees us from our boundedness and our experience of feeling imprisoned, trapped, attached or hung-up. Our quest is to be unshackled from this entrapment.

3. **From fragmentation to wholeness**

   We started this journey with a feeling of disintegration, fragmentation and a lack of synchronicity. Our quest is a journey from fragmented, scattered and dispersed living to finding ways to bring about unification, collection and wholeness.

4. **From separation to oneness**

   Living authentically can also be experienced as a movement from a divided, illogical state of consciousness to an inclusive, unified state of consciousness. The process of restoring a divided way of living starts with blending and integrating the polarities of your true being. The journey is often a struggle with and a coming to terms with your shadow, your dark side. This taming often happens through love, rather than conquering it with force.

5. **From being on a journey to arriving at the destination**

   The ever-changing flux of life's events as a journey or path is an almost universal experience. Many people experience their authentication as a journey to another land, across a river, up a mountain, through a wilderness or into the depths of the earth or the ocean. When you make the decision to discover your authentic self, to find the true core of your being, it is like a departure on a journey. This journey goes into your unknown interior landscapes, away from the safe contours of the conventional social world.

6. **From being in exile to coming home**

   The sense of being in the wrong place, of a mistake that occurred, of being a stranger, is an extremely widespread experience. We embark on our journey when we become aware of the exiled or alienated condition we are in. This is a necessary first step to returning to the homeward journey.

7. **From seed to flowering tree**

   The unfolding of your authentic self from the present, ordinary state of mindfulness to the full extension of what is possible could be compared to the growth and flowering of a tree.

8. **From death to rebirth**

   People on a journey of transformation often feel and sense that they are dying and then become reborn. When you feel that you have died, there is an end to your self-understanding that has been in existence up to that time. This is a very radical and total transformation. Such an experience brings about a radically new and different perspective and attitude about life, and a totally fresh, innocent outlook, like that of a child.

Going Meta has taken you on a journey. Your personal transformation was a deeply unique and nuanced experience. You have now discovered which one of the above descriptions resonated most with your experience.

Explore this change further by asking yourself the following question: What new identity has risen from the event that I would like to experiment with?

Try on the new identity by giving it a name and visualise yourself as the new identity. Challenge (or stop) beliefs and thoughts that criticise this new identity.

12 things to *quit* right now and 12 things to start with right now

On this quest, *Going Meta* tried to help you to stop doing 12 things – as explained in the 12 weeks of the journey.

Read through the list below and become aware of what you resonate with and where you feel resistance.

Stop running away from or towards something, anything.

Stop doubting your right to be.

Stop needing someone else to make you feel you.

Stop yearning for affection.

Stop denying who you grew to be.

Stop down-playing your qualities.

Stop trusting anyone or anything but yourself.

Stop fearing your contribution.

Stop doubting what to do with your life.

Stop telling everyone else what to do.

Stop pretending you are someone else.

Stop renouncing (refusing to recognise) your roots.

12 things to start with right now

From today ...

I will follow my passion

I will start enjoying my place in life

I will start feeling comfortable with myself

I will start loving my fellows

I will start embracing my becoming

I will start facilitating my talents

I will start exploring my inner wisdom

I will start feeling I am a gift to others

I will start following life's opportunities

I will start doing things together

I will start showing who I really am

I will start acknowledging my roots

A sense of rootedness: Paul

One rainy winter's day in Cape Town, I found myself sitting with Paul. He was preparing to fly to India again as part of a panel that had to interview new people for an IT development team. The international brand that he was working for was moving the IT shop that he was part of from Cape Town to India. The consequence for those not prepared to relocate to India, himself included, was losing their jobs.

He smiled and we both started reminiscing over the past year. "It started with that question of mine: Why do I always feel as if I have to earn my position in life?" he remembered.

"That's when you suggested we go back into my history, and I discovered that I was the child that felt a bit unwanted. My mother had only planned two children. She miscarried and then my brother was born. I came after him, the third one. Through my whole life I always felt as if I was just a replacement."

He continued, "And in that process of looking up my past, I discovered that my grandfather was a well-known photographer. Earlier I had a whole bunch of hobbies, and I did not complete anything, but now I've been enjoying this creative side of me and I've been exploring photography even more. I've become very passionate about it. And I am persisting with it.

"To know where I am coming from created a sense of rootedness. Now I tend to be more assertive, which created a sense of confidence as well. The other day, when we were really in the valley of the change curve, I could leave my role and go and help out in another role. And I wasn't concerned about my role. I just knew that I could help the team.

"That is also why I am going to India. Some people are saying, 'Oh, they expect of us to hire our replacements'. I'm sorry, I simply won't do that. The majority of the people have a more emotionally mature view and are saying this is something we have to do; it's been asked of us. I think we don't really have to do it, but we want to do the right thing. We are even developing training material to guide the new people. So I think that is a good sign!"

Task: Ask why questions

- If you often think about the intangible influences from out there, ask yourself: Why do I find "belonging to" so important?
- If you almost never think about the intangible influences from out there, ask yourself: Why do I not care about "how it should be"?

Reflection: Checking in on my origin

- What is the ONE thing that is different in your life at the end of this journey?
- Where do you need to be more "gritty" in life to protect your new-found identity?
- Which of the "12 things to start with right now" did you commit to start doing?
- How do you plan to continue on this journey?
- What have you discovered about the roots you are called to embody? Find a symbol that will remind you of your roots and your new-found identity. Display it somewhere so that it can serve as a daily reminder of your special roots.

For the more adventurous

- **Build an archetype »** Create a set of archetypes, or ideal examples, to help you explore how you see the world.

- **Personal altar »** Build a personal altar. This is a highly personal project that will help to connect you to your spiritual side and honour your resilience.

- **Family tree »** Create a family tree of strength. This exercise honours those around you who support you. Paint those close to you who offer you the strength you need.

- **Recycled art »** Make art out of recycled items. You can reuse old items that have meaning to you or just re-purpose something that is lying around. Either way, you'll get insight into how you can reshape and re-evaluate life. Use a found or made object as a paintbrush. Whether it is something sharp or something soft, make your own artistic tool and use it to express what you are feeling.

Postscript

I read the manuscript of the book for the last time before it went to the printers, as part of a feedback group. This day, we were doing a mindfulness exercise. The theme was about rootedness. We were standing barefoot outside.

André, the guy who was guiding the meditation, asked us to think of ourselves as a tree.

He invited us to think about the following questions: Where in this world does your tree stand? How does this tree experience its right to exist and to be who you are right now? How do you experience your place in this world? Where are you in this world?

He played beautiful music. I could hear the birds in the garden. I was trying to see myself as a tree. Out of nowhere a picture of a quiver tree came to me. At first I was a bit disappointed because this is not a lavish green tree.

Why would I think of such a tree? And then I remembered that two days ago I saw photos of quiver trees. I wanted to dismiss the trees as a recent memory. I thought it was not something significant. But then I decided to try and receive the quiver tree and see what happens.

I felt emotional. Then it dawned on me: I am a child of the Karoo.

I was born in a town called Williston. This small town is situated in the middle of South Africa in a semi-desert region called the Karoo.

This is a place that has survived many droughts. Plants here need to be able to have roots that can draw enough water to survive.

The plants that survive here can store small amounts of water in their leaves.

Graphically, their silhouettes make wonderful pictures against the sunset.

I re-discovered at that moment that this is where I come from!

This is where Life gave me my position in the world, the fourth of six children of the local pastor and his wife. My father served in the small rural church, built with local rocks.

This was a very close-knit farming community that supported each other through hardship. It was this same community that supported my parents when my Down syndrome sister was born, adopting her as their own.

While still standing barefoot, I experienced my roots as the quiver tree.

And the roots grew stronger and deeper until they were no longer my roots. I felt the energy of generations far beyond my own life. I was rooted in generations long before me. I felt connected, firstly to my own parents and then to their parents and their parents ...

The waves of doubt that flushed through me while writing this book made way for this knowledge that I am not alone in this. I am fine. It is good. We will survive all hardship.

I also trust that the ancient theory we are using has survived many generations and many droughts. I had to write this book – standing in this place in this world, rooted from the origin, from the source inside. The wisdom came through the ages.

Therefore, my hope is that this book will provide a playground for people to discover their authentic selves. My hope is that this book will support them to collaborate freely, connect with love and be the gift they are supposed to be, and to show this with pride while standing in the roots of their trees.

With this book I offer you a gift that I have received from many before and around us.

Acknowledgements

First acknowledgement: Marc Grond

I am writing this in Paris after a week-long visit to Marc Grond and his wife Marli at their small farm in Satagnat, France. Our friendship started a few years ago. He came to South Africa to train coaches in the use of Transmind's awareness tool called the Organic ScoreCard©. I was part of the first group. The whole idea of measuring, knowing and thinking about one's awareness was just mind-blowing.

Out of that first contact a friendship and partnership developed.

We are deeply indebted to Marc and his ideas about Organic Theory and the Organic ScoreCard©. This book would not have been possible without it. This is a repackaging of his basic theory into a personal journey. The aspects and descriptions of awareness we use come from his Organic Theory.

Marc lives life authentically. He receives insights through studies, silence, working with his hands, hardship, discussions and research. He shares this freely.

On the last day of our visit, while a group of us was meeting inside, he was cutting down trees with an electric saw to provide firewood for the coming winter – deeply in tune with genuine living.

Marc started our first day of training with a quote from Antoine de Saint-Exupéry, author of *Le Petit Prince*: "If you want to build a ship, don't drum up the men and women to gather wood, divide the work, and give orders. Instead, teach them to yearn for the vast and endless sea."

Marc, you have awakened a yearning for authentic living in us.

We thank you for this. You are a gift to us and to the whole world.

Second acknowledgement: Julia Cameron

I (Nico) have been journaling on and off my whole life. Many years ago, someone gave me Julia Cameron's The Artist's Way as a gift. My wife Elsa was the first to pick it up and start doing the daily exercises. A year later, I also took up the challenge. After struggling to start, I embarked on the 12-week programme of self-exploration. And the book and life did not disappoint me.

A few years ago I (Elsa) was advised by my therapist to embark on the 12-week journey outlined in Julia Cameron's The Artist's Way. I fell in love with this journey and everything that happened. It became a sacred space every morning as I was writing the morning pages and every Sunday as I read the next chapter. There were ups and downs, but mostly I enjoyed and persevered. Then the 12 weeks ended and I really struggled to keep going with this journey. Somehow, it became difficult to put time and energy aside for this "inside work". It was as if the structure of the book guided and supported me so that I could rest and play within it.

Julia, many years later, the structure and the inspiration of your book supported and guided me to write this book. Thank you.

Third acknowledgement: Keith Cunningham

In 2013, in the middle of London, Nico practised one of his habits. Walking into a bookshop, he went to a field of expertise he knew very little about and picked a random book. He chose *The Soul of Screenwriting: On Writing, Dramatic Truth, and Knowing Yourself* by Keith Cunningham, and have been studying it ever since. When we went through a dark night of the soul, this book guided us on our journey. The author showed us the obstacles, signposts and challenges, but also the hope and joy of the hero's journey. It became our sense-making tool.

We did not use the book to write a screenplay, but it accompanied us on a dramatic journey of getting to know ourselves. Even though Cunningham did not discover the hero's journey, he unlocked it for us.

We are deeply indebted to him. He saved our lives, and inspired the weekly goal post on the flow of the journey.

Fourth acknowledgement: Jackie Plank

In this book, when we write about a guide, we have a specific type of person in mind. You can only learn from someone if that person deeply loves you. We have the privilege of having a Jackie in our life. Everyone should have a Jackie.

We have been going to her on and off for the past eight years. She has been our guide, companion, cheerleader, support system, motivator, guru, coach, teacher, healer and friend on our journey.

We almost never tell her how much she has meant and is still meaning to us. We go to her, sit down and download, complain, think out loud and resist what is happening to us. And she gives perspective, guidance and comfort. Most of all, she helps us see the exciting journey called life on which we have embarked.

She saw this book three years before it happened.

Jackie, this is for you. Words cannot express our thanks.

Fifth acknowledgement

Nico and I realise that this book has been nurtured by the roots of all who have lived before, around and through us. We remember Koos Marais and James Simpson, our fathers who each stood their ground in their own way. We want to salute our mothers, Alta Marais and Marianna Simpson. You gave us life. We build on your legacy.

We also remember Huibrie Marais, Elsa's late sister, who shaped all of us in a special way. At Huibrie's remembrance service, Elsa and Huibrie's brother Frederick said the following: "Humanly speaking, our sister lacked the intellectual abilities of her siblings. Yet, she leaves a much more far reaching legacy."

We treasure the families that deeply root us: Aletta en Ian Bruyns, Elmien en Pieter Kloppers, Frederick and Anita Marais, Kobus en Marelize Marais, Bettie Marais, Jacques and Lorraine Simpson, JC Simpson, and Marie Olivier.

We are deeply indebted to friends for helping us finalise this endeavour. Hester Fourie, thank you for the first read and for your kind and supportive feedback. Amanda Matthee, thank you for your editing and validation of the project. The time and effort you have put into this project is a true gift to us. Lizanne Murison, we knew from the beginning we wanted you to do apply your beautiful and intelligent design to this manuscript – and you did!

We appreciate everyone who, week after week, journeyed through the early versions of the manuscript with us. Your feedback, insights and stories found their way back into the manuscript. (Some were altered to protect the contributors' identities.) We take off our hats to all those who have contributed to the stories in this book. We would therefore like to acknowledge the contributions of the following friends, coaches, coachees, colleagues and fellow travellers:

Adele Peloi, Adriana Botha, Alan and Kathryn O'Regan, Alet Ackermann, Anchen Pienaar, André Kilian, Arno de Vries, Arno Loots, Astrid van Tongeren, Barnard Steyn, Belinda Bosman, Blom and Dalene Gelderblom, Brigitte Muller, Carl and Jacque Pretorius, Carol May, Carol Richards, Carol Schroeder, Chantell Holland, Chris and Suzanne Bateman, Chris Harris, Christiaan Stroebel, Cordi van Niekerk, Craig Aitchison, Dalene Crafford, David Dalziel, Delmarie van Oudtshoorn, Densher de Koker, Duncan Macdonald, Duncan McGregor, Elsabe du Plessis, Elza Bresler, Erone van Rensburg, Febbie Malherbe, Garth Samaai, Gielie and Marie Loubser, Gillian Geldenhuys, Giselle Deuchar, Gregg MacIntyre, Gwen Gous, Heloise van der Mescht, Hendri Fourie, Hennie and Heleen Meyer, Iain Williamson, Ilse Laubscher, Ilse Nunes, Jaco Burger, Jampie Nel, Jandirk and Erna Pronk, Jeanie le Roux, Jenny Coetsee, Johnson Idesoh, Joke Lodewijk, Jonathan Orford, Judith Kotze, Julian Joshua, Kara Naseema, Karen Swart, Karin Hall, Kelly-Ann Karma, Kerissa Varma, Kevin Cilliers, Khanya Blou, Lenois and Karmia Stander, Lorelei Jensen, Louisa Botes, Lulu Bräsler, Lulu Larche, Maartin Post, Malcolm Fielies, Mari Bosch, Marianne and Tinus Loots, Mariette van der Merwe and Hans de Kwaadsteniet, Marinus Loots, Marius Nel, Mark Daries, Marlene Cronjé, Marlie Grond, Marlise Mouton, Martin Slabber, Monene Murray, Moses Mareya, Nadene Botto, Nadia Mohamed, Nathania Hendriks, Nicolaas Vercuiel, Nommiselo Twalo, Paul Knauer,

Philip du Plessis, Philipp Dietmann, Piet and Karen Burger, Piet Kubheka, Pieter Kloppers, Pieter Malherbe, Pieter van der Walt, Retha and Nieldane Stodart, Riana and Nigel Martin, Riana Fourie, Rocco and Lizette Nel, Sarina Cronjé, Sebastian Whelan, Siegfried Louw, Simangele Sealetsa, Steve Hattingh, Suzan Strauss, Tags Moodley, Theunis Botha, Thys and Janie Wentzel, Ulandi Greyling, Ulvi Guliyev, Werner van Rensburg, Wim and Loulize de Klerk, and Zeldi Hall.

A final word of acknowledgement and thanks: We have sourced the activities, examples and suggestions in this book from courses we have attended over the years, people we have encountered along the way, and websites we have visited. While writing the book, we became aware that we did not know the sources of everything we have included. If you come across something that we did not acknowledge sufficiently, please be so kind as to contact us so that we can acknowledge your contribution.

ADDENDUM 1

Emotional Grid

I feel at peace

or I feel …
Anxious to survive
Anxious not to recognise myself

I feel united

or I feel …
Anxious to be lost
Anxious not to feel united

I feel grounded

or I feel …
Anxious about not feeling at ease
Anxious that I'm not grounded

I feel loved

or I feel …
Anxious not to be loved
Anxious not to be in a relationship

I feel self-accepting

or I feel …
Anxious not to understand myself
Anxious not to be normal

I feel facilitated

or I feel …
Anxious not to find a place
Anxious to have no place

I feel self-recognised

or I feel …
Anxious not to feel my wisdom
Anxious not to know

I feel acknowledged

or I feel …
Anxious not to be accepted
Anxious for not knowing what people need from me

I feel flexible

or I feel …
Anxious to be prepared
Anxious to know what the next step is

I feel involved

or I feel …
Anxious not to be allowed to participate
Anxious not to be able to provide input

I feel visible

or I feel …
Anxious not to be seen
Anxious for not knowing what others expect of me

I feel rooted

or I feel …
Anxious for being pushed out
Anxious for not being

ADDENDUM 2

Journaling Examples

Example 1

Captain's log » "I did not bring work home yesterday." (the facts)

Diary » "I did not bring work home yesterday which normally would make me feel guilty, but yesterday I felt free." (a shift)

Debrief » "I had been so stressed for such a long time I felt it was going to depress me, so I did not bring work home yesterday which normally would make me feel guilty, but yesterday I felt free." (emotions)

Example 2

Captain's log » "I had a conversation with my boss. She asked me to redo the report." (the facts)

Diary » "I had a conversation with my boss. She asked me to redo the report which usually makes me upset and this happened again." (no shift)

Debrief » "I had a nasty conversation with that awful woman that is unfortunately my boss. She asked me with a stupid grin to redo the report which always makes me heavily upset and this happened again. I hate her!" (emotions)

Example 3

Captain's log » "My colleague came in today in a crying mood." (the facts)

Diary » "My colleague came in today in a crying mood. I immediately felt sorry for her and stopped smiling." (a shift)

Debrief » "My sweetest colleague came in today in an alarming crying mood. I of course immediately felt sooo sorry for her, I stopped smiling and was emotionally touched." (emotions)

Example 4

Captain's log » "I said no." (the facts)

Diary » "I am taking control of my private life and to my surprise that feels good!" (a shift)

Debrief » "It feels victoriously liberating to push back on all these stupid demands." (emotions)

Example 5

Captain's log » "I had a long discussion with my boss." (the facts)

Diary » "The discussion with my boss played out differently. Happily she seemed to be more open to my suggestions." (a shift)

Debrief » "I finally felt appreciated and listened to for the first time here! Can you believe that?" (emotions)

ADDENDUM 3

Organic Awareness Theory

Organic Theory is an invitation for you to grow your potential and acknowledge your inner needs.

Organic Growth underlines the fact that people are living organisms. Down to cellular level, we as organisms are developing under the influence of environment and time.

Organic Growth means that every cell is growing, and that growth, by nature, is weighed and balanced.

It also means that each component is co-evolving in conjunction with all other components. Each cell is influencing all other cells while also being influenced by these cells. Optimal life and awareness means that a person can move freely, unhindered by physical or mental numbness, damage or obstacles. It means development, play and work.

To help people reach their full potential, it makes sense to first gain insight into where they are in terms of their development.

- Where is this person holding back?
- Where has this person slowed down or lost mobility?

This will give us insight into this person's strengths and weaknesses. Based on this, someone can form relationships and become productive. Guidance can then be based on that person's own perspective. It is not based on the environment and the position taken by that person.

All behaviour stems from awareness

Awareness is divided into 12 "windows" through which one can look at the world. In Organic Theory these windows are called "domains". They are the "windows" upon which we build our vision of the opportunities in the world around us. If we do not see the "windows" we have opened and the ones that are closed, our behaviour will stay the same.

Domains and their combinations are crosscuts of our awareness. These crosscuts are controlled by our brain in three different ways: survival, connection and trust.

Once we have insight into this brain functioning, we can understand, explain and predict our behaviour. We can even contribute to behavioural improvement in our environment.

Human beings try to construct the most appropriate way to deal with life. We develop a bundle of experiences, interpretations and images. Organic Theory calls this bundle a life strategy. The life strategy that people use consists of parts from a time in their past when they were useful and effective. However, today, these parts can block meaningful behaviour and hamper optimal growth.

The tool that Organic Theory uses to offer an "X-ray" of this life strategy is the Organic ScoreCard© (OSC).

The OSC makes our brain strategy visible in the 12 domains. It gives a picture that shows you where you really want to grow, why you are obstructing your own growth (old obstacles) and what you can do to step into this natural longing for growth.

A life strategy is always neutral. The context determines the extent to which it helps you.

Brain functioning: three dominant systems

Brain stem or reptile brain

The brain stem offers survival opportunities in situations when our lives are in danger. It is popularly known as the fight-or-flight mode of our body. It also refers to freeze, hide and submit.

All emotions in their absolute origin stem from our fear of death. This makes our brain stem the key system in our daily caring and daring. In our lives, we seldom meet real danger of dying but our brainstem directs us anyway.

It guides us in wanting to win and hating to lose, in changing, in passion, in creating and in fearing, in being restless or unable to act.

We call this the "humanised" outcomes of the brain stem.

Limbic or mammal brain

The limbic brain evaluates who can help us to survive and who is threatening us. It gives us the ability to stabilise. It assures our lives through finding the most helpful company on our life journey. It shapes our emotions into feelings that are acceptable in our human encounters. It makes us predictable and understandable. It helps us to understand others, to make friends, and to be loyal and reasonable.

But it also has the capability of holding on tight, of not letting go, and of being rigid, which can cause trouble in life.

Neocortex or human brain

The neocortex creates the opportunity to surpass your survival intuition and let go of inappropriate life strategies. Hope and belief, unconditional love, abstract thinking, and time and space insights derive from this. It is our non-emotional system, and it is not occupied with surviving. It gives words and reasons to our survival-oriented behaviour that is dominant in most of human life.

ADDENDUM 4

Research on interventions

Unit for Innovation and Transformation (Ekklesia), Stellenbosch University

Researchers: Dr Frederick Marais (advisor) and Ankia du Plooy

Eighteen months after we started an intervention at a global company, the project moved abroad. Most of the people knew there was a 90% chance that the Cape Town office would close down. They were offered severance packages. Most were looking for new jobs. Among the chaos new opportunities surfaced. One of the opportunities being that the head office in the USA wanted us to come and do the same intervention there. But, for the proposal we needed scientific proof that what we did was successful.

We decided to do the research. We got a partner at Stellenbosch University. We did 20 structured interviews with participants who went through the intervention. We recorded the interviews and had these transcribed. The researchers at the university analysed it.

I wanted to know what worked and what did not work. What was the impact , and what did we do that really made a difference?

Here is a summary of the report.

Introduction

Clariact, a Cape Town-based company that offers training and coaching interventions to enhance the performance of teams, designed an intervention called the Clariact Intervention. This intervention can be used, among others, to support and enhance the agile methodologies used in companies. The intervention is underpinned by various human development theories and coaching frameworks. It uses both coaching sessions and facilitated workshops to enhance performance.

The Unit for Innovation and Transformation at Stellenbosch University was approached by Elsa Simpson to conduct a qualitative investigation to gain insight into the participants' experiences of the intervention.

The data collection method consisted of structured face-to-face interviews with 18 participants. The interviews were voice-recorded and transcribed to allow for thematic content analysis.

The aim of this study was to determine the impact of the outcomes of the intervention on participants and their work environments, and to use these outcomes in the planning and implementation of further interventions.

How did the Clariact Intervention enhance and support agile methodologies in the IT environment?

In essence, the intervention helped participants to acquire the emotional maturity and confidence to optimise their outputs in fast-moving agile environments. The following themes emerged from the thematic content analysis of the one-on-one interviews with participants in the Clariact Intervention, as applied in agile environments.

Personal growth through increased self-awareness and group awareness

In terms of awareness, the intervention made a significant positive impact on all the respondents. The biggest impact on a personal level was that respondents gained insight in terms of self-awareness ("I understand myself better") and group awareness ("I understand the team better"; "I appreciate the different gifts of the different people"; "Without a doubt it changed my perspective"). This led to increased team cohesion and team functioning ("helped us to work more collaboratively"; "were able to make new connections"), better communication ("helped to go straight to the point") and increased outputs, which are crucial in agile environments. In essence, this helped participants to acquire emotional maturity.

Increased clarity on team roles, leading to increased confidence and empowerment of team members

Team members felt empowered in the functional roles, which created confidence that impacted personal lives as well as team functioning ("team roles were affirmed and that created more confidence"; "good understanding of the team and how they work together to become more productive"; "helped working with different teams and knowing the unique angle where to work from as well as knowing the unique energy of the different teams"). The intervention created a space in which people were able to undergo "huge shifts" in their lives. This also helped them to cope with the trauma of organisational change.

Increased team functioning and team outputs

Team members agreed that the intervention led to significantly enhanced team functioning ("less judgement in the team"; "took away the barriers and guards"; "a lot more tolerance towards the other team members"; "all are different, but the differences complement each other"; "closer relationships improved the team's functioning"; "much more collaboration and respectful interaction"; "not only black and white, also pay attention to the emotional side of people"; "the biggest team function change would definitely be understanding"; "it just made me feel more sure of what I was doing in my team, and the contribution I was making to the team").

Stronger leadership and management skills

Respondents in managerial positions commented that the tools and skills they had acquired during the intervention helped them to be better managers and leaders ("gave leaders tools to enhance their leadership style and to use in managing and creating the teams"; "helped from a management perspective to understand how to engage with different individuals and different teams").

Ideal fit with agile methodologies in IT environments

The intervention supported the ability of team leaders to put together high-performing and self-sufficient teams ("better communication enhanced performance and individual discipline"; "could form teams to fit each other and complement each other to improved performance"; "for agile methodologies to work you really need to understand the people in the team that you're working with as well as possible, because it requires a lot more interaction between individuals than any other process"; "one of the things agility strives to do is to take the personal individual qualities, and take them into account in the way teams function; the intervention certainly supported that and helped the team to be able to use the individual traits they had better, and to understand each other better, which is very central to agile"; "build trust in the teams, which is something from the agile environment you really try to build from the beginning".)

Enhanced ability to deal with change

A significant number of participants made mention of their new approach to change and their ability to handle change better after the intervention. The intervention was particularly valuable to a number of IT people working for a company in the process of restructuring ("a company going through restructuring and retrenchments is like a slow-motion car crash ... and the intervention gave first aid"; "handled change more maturely and used it as a growth opportunity"; "because they went through deep change on a personal level that positively impacted them, to be in a better position to handle the organisational change").

Efficiency of the intervention

The intervention used a combination of one-on-one coaching sessions ("appreciated the deep listening"; "one-on-ones deepened the whole journey") and facilitated workshops to enhance performance. Prior to the actual intervention, participants were invited to do a number of online assessments, including the Organic ScoreCard. This was well received by the participants ("you could drive straight to the point and didn't spend months sitting in therapy until you eventually stumbled on it. So it was really a tool to give you a map, and then through discussion and so on it facilitated us getting to the issue really quickly ... it saved a lot of time, the assessment [helped us] to go straight to where we actually needed to work"; "I was surprised that out of so few questions you could get such an accurate picture"). Participants also commented on the integrated approach to performance enhancement ("was not only about work, but an integrated process about life"; "helped to evolve as a person"; "positive towards the company who made the investment"; "this was by far the most insightful exercise I think I've ever done").

ADDENDUM 5

Group discussion guide

ONE: Recognising the full worth of my existence

Checking in

- Split into pairs and answer one or more of the following questions:
  - What was your highlight of the week?
  - What were you up against this week?
  - Where did life affirm or disrupt your journey this week?
- Return to the group and give each person 30 seconds to share an insight or understanding with the larger group.

Journey: Starting the journey

Let's reflect on the integration of what happened in your life during this week's journey. Discuss the following questions:

- In facing the beginning of your transformation journey, what pressures did you experience?
- What were the clues of your authentic self that evolved? Share the clues.
- What was the call to action or challenge that emerged through this new beginning towards authenticity?

Awareness

Use the following questions to guide your discussion of each aspect of this week's awareness.

A. Be alert to the possibilities that life offers

Who or what validated your position and contribution during the past week? Share the story.

B. I do what I do because I am who I am

Share your reflections on your different positions in life and the authority it has given you.

C. **Embrace the givenness of life**

Which of the suggestions to receive the givenness of life have helped you to experience peace of mind?

Main insight

What has been your main insight or learning from this week?

TWO: Recognising the full worth of my inside

Checking in

- Split into pairs and answer one or more of the following questions:
  - What was your highlight of the week?
  - What were you up against this week?
  - Where did life affirm or disrupt your journey this week?
- Return to the group and give each person 30 seconds to share an insight or understanding with the larger group.

Journey: Call to action

In which of the following three ways did your call to action unfold during the past week?

Call from within » Where in your life do you identify with Little Hans's experience of outgrowing your "hut/home", and where do you need to reinvent? Tell the story.

Call from without » Who or what challenged you this week to focus on your strengths and gifts, and use these in a new way or apply these to a challenging project or job? Describe the circumstances and timing.

Call from below » Did any major "mistakes" happen this week? How did this guide you towards your call to your authentic self?

How can you use this "significant" mistake to change the direction of your life?

Awareness

A. **Born beautifully – reinventing myself**

Tell the story about reinventing yourself in the past. How does that inspire you?

B. **Reliable bearer of care**

Manifesto: If you have written a manifesto, read your favourite sentence.

If you struggled to write a manifesto, read through the *Create a personal manifesto* questions and formulate one sentence out loud.

C. **Radiate inner confidence**

What was your favourite exercise this week? Explain why.

Main insight

What has been your main insight or learning from this week?

THREE: Recognising the full worth of my grounding

Checking in

- Split into pairs and answer one or more of the following questions:
  - What was your highlight of the week?
  - What were you up against this week?
  - Where did life affirm or disrupt your journey this week?
- Return to the group and give each person 30 seconds to share an insight or understanding with the larger group.

Journey: Overcoming fears

Let's reflect on the integration of what has happened in your life during this week's journey. Discuss the following questions:

What fears have you been confronted with during this week? Share what you feel comfortable with.

Did you meet any "threshold guardians" this week? What is your growth challenge?

Awareness

Use the following questions to guide your discussion about each aspect of this week's awareness.

A. **Certainty is an illusion – be open to the here and now**

   What is it that you have to let go of this week?

B. **Practising peace of mind**

   Where do you fly too low? (Icarus story)

   Where do you settle for less than what you are capable of?

   What excuses did you make? (See *List of excuses*)

   If you did not mark the above excuses, take a moment now and mark one in each section. Read them out loud.

C. **Acceptance – it is what it is**

   Where do you find yourself on Henry Nouwen's continuum from loneliness to solitude?

   Share your thoughts.

Main insight

What has been your main insight or learning from this week?

FOUR: Recognising the full worth of my friendship

Checking in

- Split into pairs and answer one or more of the following questions:
  - What was your highlight of the week?
  - What were you up against this week?
  - Where did life affirm or disrupt your journey this week?
- Return to the group and give each person 30 seconds to share an insight or understanding with the larger group.

Journey: Meeting your mentor

Could you spot a mentor or new community supporting you on your journey? Explain who they are and how they support you.

Awareness

A. Don't let friends do silly things – alone

Have you reached out to "date" or get to know a new person in your life? If yes, tell the story.

If no, consider why not and explore a few names and commit to contacting one person.

B. Be a relationship builder

Explore the *Create Connection* list. What did you choose and how did it play out?

If not, read through it now and choose one to explore. Tell the group how you are going to do this.

C. Accept without reserve

Did you manage to appreciate someone in your immediate environment at home or in your workplace? Share the effect it had.

Main insight

What has been your main insight or learning from this week?

FIVE: Recognising the full worth of my contribution

Checking in

- Split into pairs and answer one or more of the following questions:
  - What was your highlight of the week?
  - What were you up against this week?
  - Where did life affirm or disrupt your journey this week?
- Return to the group and give each person 30 seconds to share an insight or understanding with the larger group.

Journey: Crossing a threshold

Are you busy rewriting your story? What is the theme of this new chapter or phase in your life?

What is the new identity evolving?

Awareness

A. Relevance is a bitch

Have you tried to keep quiet and truly listen to people? Explain the outcome and new insights.

In the story of the soup pot grabber, with whom did you identify – the soup pot grabber, the other siblings or the parents? Explain why.

B. Not hype but quality

Did you pose some of the relevance-centred questions to your customers or the people around you? What did you learn about your service or behaviour?

If not, choose one or two questions now and ask the group members about your contribution in the group.

C. Lighthouses just stand there and shine

Take a moment and write down the names of all the members in the group. Write down one appreciative sentence about each group member's contribution. Let all the group members share their sentences.

Main insight

What insight did you gain this week about your gift to the environment? Share.

SIX: Recognising the full worth of my creativity

Checking in

- Split into pairs and answer one or more of the following questions:
  - What was your highlight of the week?
  - What were you up against this week?
  - Where did life affirm or disrupt your journey this week?
- Return to the group and give each person 30 seconds to share an insight or understanding with the larger group.

Journey: Obstacles and tests

What did you experience, or how did you experience the energy shift?

Was it a moment of grace, a moment of enlightenment or a mind-f**k moment?

Tell the story of what happened.

Awareness

A. Truth and knowledge are within me

Where or when did you experience your wisdom or creativity breaking through to solve a problem or creating something new?

B. Standing in the wisdom of many generations

Share a story of how you learned from a mistake you had made.

C. Open to my inner source of knowledge

Pause and reflect on all the wisdom you have gained so far on this journey. Share and celebrate the inner wisdom that is serving you.

Main insight

What has been your main insight or learning from this week?

SEVEN: Recognising the full worth of my playground

Checking in

- Split into pairs and answer one or more of the following questions:
  - What was your highlight of the week?
  - What were you up against this week?
  - Where did life affirm or disrupt your journey this week?
- Return to the group and give each person 30 seconds to share an insight or understanding with the larger group.

Journey: Final preparations before taking a leap

Share the clues of your authentic self that have become clear to you. What resistance or struggles do you experience from living in this new way? Share.

Awareness

A. Push and pull towards an optimal environment

Which one of the emotional symptoms did you recognise as a road sign to get unstuck? Explain.

B. Creating order and tidying up

What changes do you need to make in your environment to help you rise to your potential? What have you already done? What do you plan to do?

C. Life conspires to help me

Where in your life do you experience flow? Explain.

Main insight

What has been your main insight or learning from this week?

EIGHT: Recognising the full worth of my biography

Checking in

- Split into pairs and answer one or more of the following questions:
  - What was your highlight of the week?
  - What were you up against this week?
  - Where did life affirm or disrupt your journey this week?
- Return to the group and give each person 30 seconds to share an insight or understanding with the larger group.

Journey: Face to face with my deepest fears

Which "monster" do you need to slay or what difficulty do you need to overcome to embrace the evolving new you?

Awareness

A. **Seeking self-knowledge and self-realisation**

Share the insights from your lifeline exercise. What is the name of your monster and/or your new story?

B. **Investigating to solve "the mystery of me"**

Which story plot theme did you identify with (See *Choose your own story plot*) and why?

C. **I accept all the puzzle pieces of my story**

Take turns and validate the brave stories of all the group members. Let one or two people volunteer to affirm each person in the group.

Main insight

What has been your main insight or learning from this week?

NINE: Recognising the full worth of my future

Checking in

- Split into pairs and answer one or more of the following questions:
  - What was your highlight of the week?
  - What were you up against this week?
  - Where did life affirm or disrupt your journey this week?
- Return to the group and give each person 30 seconds to share an insight or understanding with the larger group.

Journey: Deep transformation

What is the treasure that you have found on this journey? Explain.

How did you celebrate it or how can we celebrate your treasure in the group?

How do you plan to protect the new-found treasure? Explain.

Awareness

A. **Finding life at the edge of my comfort zone**

Can you think of a successful transition in your life? What were your insights?
If not, take a moment, identify a transformation and then share this with the group.

B. **Mapping future possibilities – chess is not for anxious souls**

"No plan survives the enemy!" What does this mean to you in your life? Share.

C. **Calm regardless of what is coming my way**

With which one of the shapeshifters did you identify and why? Share.

Main insight

What has been your main insight or learning from this week?

TEN: Recognising the full worth of my collaboration

Checking in

- Split into pairs and answer one or more of the following questions:
  - What was your highlight of the week?
  - What were you up against this week?
  - Where did life affirm or disrupt your journey this week?

- Return to the group and give each person 30 seconds to share an insight or understanding with the larger group.

Journey: Tempted onto side roads

In the last "chase scene" of your journey, what "side roads" tempted you to escape from this new path or goal? Tell the story.

Awareness

A. **Take control – provide direction**

How did "staying in the adult mindset" assist you this week? Discuss. If you have not practised this mindset yet, decide where you could use this skill in the future. Share.

B. **Anchors at the core of the team**

Take a moment and let everyone share a positive affirmation of themselves.

C. **Trust is better than control**

Reflect on where you could use "Don't take it personal". Share.

Main insight

What has been your main insight or learning from this week?

ELEVEN: Recognising the full worth of my outside

Checking in

- Split into pairs and answer one or more of the following questions:
    - What was your highlight of the week?
    - What were you up against this week?
    - Where did life affirm or disrupt your journey this week?
- Return to the group and give each person 30 seconds to share an insight or understanding with the larger group.

Journey: Struggling to stay authentic

What symbolises your final challenge on this journey? What can you celebrate so far? Share.

Awareness

A. **Enthusiasm brings movement**

   How are you different or how do you "stand out" in life? How does this serve you? Share.

B. **Determined to show the best**

   Have you come across the not-good-enough monster in your life? How do you deal with this monster?

C. **Embodying invitation**

   In what ways were you kind to people this week? Share.

Main insight

What has been your main insight or learning from this week?

TWELVE: Recognising the full worth of my origin

Checking in

- Split into pairs and answer one or more of the following questions:
    - What was your highlight of the week?
    - What were you up against this week?
    - Where did life affirm or disrupt your journey this week?
- Return to the group and give each person 30 seconds to share an insight or understanding with the larger group.

Journey: Returning home a changed person

What is the ONE thing that is different in your life at the end of this journey?

Awareness

A. **Bend things seen as straight lines**

Where do you need to be more "gritty" in life to protect your new-found identity?

B. **First among equals**

What is the ONE thing now that will embody your authentic self?

C. **Stand for eternal truth**

Which of the "12 things to start with right now" did you commit to start doing?

Main insight

What has been your main insight or learning from this week?

Ending

Take time and appreciate and validate each other for the gift of travelling together during the past few weeks.

www.ingramcontent.com/pod-product-compliance
Lightning Source LLC
Chambersburg PA
CBHW081132090426
42737CB00018B/3302